THE NEW RUSSIAN POETS: 1953 to 1968

The New Russian Poets

1953–1968

AN ANTHOLOGY

*Selected, Edited and Translated
by* GEORGE REAVEY

Bilingual Edition

October House Inc.　New York

ACKNOWLEDGMENTS

The first five Yevtushenko poems are taken from *The Poetry of Yevgeny Yevtushenko*, October House Inc., New York. Some poems have previously appeared in *Evergreen Review*, *Gentleman's Quarterly*, *Mademoiselle*, and *Modern European Poetry*, Bantam Books Inc., New York.

Published by October House Inc.
55 West 13th Street, New York
Copyright © 1966, 1968 by George Reavey
All rights reserved
Library of Congress catalog card number 66–15272
Printed in the United States of America
First Edition 1966
Second Printing December 1967
Designed by Bert Clarke

Contents

The New Russian Poets and the Crisis of Belief

Since the "Golden Age" of Alexander Pushkin (1799–1837) and Mikhail Lermontov (1814–1841), Russians have always taken great pride in their poetic achievement as the art closest to the national heartbeat, to the emotions and aspirations of their ideal national selves. It was only in the nineteenth century that they began to discover and revel in the beauty, musical enchantment, and genuine validity of their own language which, thanks to Pushkin's having forged a more supple and musical verbal medium, soon ended the hegemony exercised until then by the French language and literature as the staple diet of the educated minority. But the ascending Russian Muse also began to assume the enigmatic features of the long-suffering "Mother Russia." This was certainly the case in the poetry of N. A. Nekrasov (1821–1877). The Russian poets early developed a sense of mission, which is already present in some of Pushkin's work. As Yevgeny Yevtushenko writes in his *Precocious Autobiography*: "The poets of Russia were always warriors for the future of their native land, for the triumph of justice. The poets helped Russia to think. . . . The poets helped Russia to struggle against her tyrants."

Behind the figure of "Mother Russia" often appears a sort of Hamletian ghost of mumbled guilt and whispered retribution whom the poet-son cannot help but overhear and interpret as a call to duty. The predicament the poet may then find himself in can be summed up as follows:

> *I fear to say the change is for the better;*
> *To say it's "for the worse" is dangerous.*[1]

Behind his façade of beauty and lyrical impulse lurks a shadow, the poet soon discovers. It may be the Stepfather shadow of a Tsar Nicholas I or a Joseph Stalin, or it may be the shadow of a

---

1. Yevgeny Yevtushenko, "Letter to Yesenin."

"gunman." Thus, behind Pushkin stand Nicholas I and the Baron D'Anthès; behind Lermontov, Captain Martynov. Both D'Anthès and Martynov killed their poet-adversaries in duels. Prophetically, in Pushkin's *Evgeny Onegin* chill-hearted Evgeny had to destroy the lyrically warm, romantic poet Lensky. In Pushkin we have again the unpredictably dynamic and brutal image of "The Bronze Horseman,"[2] a personification of the ruthless State that can arbitrarily trample an individual to death. These are poetic images, ghosts out of the past, perhaps, but they are none the less real in the sense that they are dire images that have haunted Russian poetry up to the present day. Thus, in a recent poem "Lermontov," Yevgeny Yevtushenko writes:

> *In Russia poets are born*
> *With D'Anthès' bullet in their chests.*[3]

In another untitled poem on the same theme, Bella Akhmadulina asks:

> *With what shall I console those stricken*
> *by the trifling superiority of evil?*
> *Those renowned, defeated poets,*
> *who lost their lives in vain?*[4]

She finds that their "salvation" lies in "an eternally established order," in which "the triumphing boor is sentenced and condemned."

Two other poets of tragic destiny—Mayakovsky and Yesenin—haunt the imagination of many of today's young Soviet poets. In his "reverse time" passage in "Oza," Andrey Voznesensky sees the bullet "Flying out of Mayakovsky's heart. . . ."[5] In his "Mayakovsky" poem,[6] Yevtushenko asks what that poet would have done in "the year 1937," the year of the Big Purge under Stalin and concludes that he would not have kept quiet even if he had been spared. Indeed, "he left us some bullets in that re-

2. A poem of Pushkin's centering round the Falconet statue of Peter the Great in St. Petersburg.

3. *Den Poezii*. M, 1965.

4. *Struna*. M, 1962.

5. *Molodaya* Gvardia, No. 10, 1964. Also in Part IV of "Oza" in this volume.

6. *Yunost*, No. 4, 1965.

volver," Yevtushenko comments, bullets to use against "crassness, hypocrisy, and vileness." It should now be clear even from
these few examples that the "ghosts of the past" can have a very
real and immediate significance for the Russian poets of today
whose conscience has been doubly roused by the revelations about
"Stalin's crimes." Thus, the ghostly note of retribution sounds
in the lines:

> *The Muse is the child of compassion,*
> *but hatred is her nurse . . .*[7]

2. A FEW REFLECTIONS ON RUSSIAN POETRY AND THE IMPACT OF "SCIENCE"

If poetry is the soul of myth, then prose must be the foster parent
of science. It is no accident that English prose began to develop in
the age of Newton. Nor is it chance that Russian prose criticism
and fiction began to assert themselves as imported from Europe.
The spread of Russian critical thought and the rapid flowering
of the Russian novel with Gogol and Dostoyevsky, Turgenev and
Tolstoy, seemed to arrest the progress of Russian poetry for almost
half a century, though a number of poets, such as Tyutchev, Fet,
and Nekrasov, continued to write. There was also the increeping
tide of philosophical and political systems (Positivism, Socialism,
and eventually Marxism), and scientific ideas (the natural
sciences, Darwinism, the new physics), and the first rumblings in
Russia of an industrial revolution. In the nineteenth century
Russian society, which was still rather archaic in many respects,
was faced with the task of absorbing and digesting too many ideas
in too brief a space of time. As history has so far demonstrated,
this society, in the process of changing into the Soviet Union,
opted for a Russian version of Marxism as a more controlled and
more exclusive way of digesting Western civilization. It selected
to import and absorb slowly Western industrial technology and
to export rapidly its own brand of political ideas and techniques.
The imposition of a Marxist system under a one-party rule was
to have a grave effect on the course of Russian poetry, for it was
claimed that Marxism was a "science" and that literature should
be subordinated to its social directives.

---

7. Yevtushenko, "Lermontov."

In retrospect, we can already observe the impact on Russian poetry of the natural sciences and of Positivism in Turgenev's famous novel *Fathers and Sons* (1862). The "Nihilist" characters (Bazarov and Arcady) in the novel have a certain blunt way of questioning "established values" from the position of "science" and "utility," a critical attitude reminiscent of the social philosophy of the Russian critic P. I. Pisarev (1840–1868), the author of "Belinsky and Pushkin," "The Realists," and other provocative essays in the days when it became fashionable to say that "a pair of boots was of more use than the Sistine Madonna." They also have a very definite attitude of *positive* contempt for poetry which can be seen in the following passage:

Arcady came up without a word, though with a look of affectionate pity on his face, gently took away my book as he might have taken it from a child, and put another one in front of me, a German one. . . . He smiled and then went out, carrying off my Pushkin.[8]

The "German" book in this case was a "scientific treatise, *Stoff und Kraft* by Büchner. Written in the early 1860's, the passage from *Fathers and Sons* reads almost like a parody, a gentle parody of what might have happened not so gently in 1930, when the obligatory book might have been Marx's *Das Kapital*, Gorky's *Mother*, or *The Problems of Leninism* by Stalin, or in 1938, when it would have been Chapter IV of *The Short Course* (*The History of the C.P.S.U.[B]*), the chapter on "Dialectical and Historical Materialism," which was written by J. Stalin himself and in which he argues that "the science of history . . . can become as precise a science as, let us say, biology. . . ." He insisted also on "the unity of theory and practice," which was precisely the lever that was to be applied to literature and the arts in order to make of them the reflex of the general line of Communist social development. This no doubt was the culmination of a fanatical nineteenth-century acceptance and worship of a limited notion of science as the ultimate solution for all human and social problems.

But despite the "scientific" onslaught on him, Pushkin was to survive. In 1880 Dostoyevsky delivered his famous address on Pushkin as the national poet of Russia; and within twenty years

---

8. Ivan Turgenev. *Fathers and Sons*. Tr. by George Reavey. A Signet Classic. New American Library, N.Y., 1961. p. 52.

a strong poetic revival had begun. The poets associated with it were Bryusov, Blok, Ivanov, Biely (Symbolists); Gumilev, Akhmatova, Mandelshtam (Acmeists); Khlebnikov, Mayakovsky (Futurists); Pasternak, Yesenin, and others. The revival was to last almost thirty years, a revival the consequences of which are still being felt and absorbed, even after several decades of Stalinist repression, by the present generation of Soviet poets. Pasternak and Akhmatova, as we know, survived into the 1960's and played an important part in the post-Stalin revival of poetry. and Pushkin himself, after having been again "thrown overboard from the boat of contemporaneity," this time by the Russian Futurists in 1912, was to find himself officially rehabilitated and propagated for national purposes in 1936. Since then he seems to have become the second-best-selling author of pre-Revolutionary vintage throughout the Soviet Union. However, it is not Pushkin's now official status that explains his continuing sway over millions of Russians. He is, indeed, the national poet and has an appeal and power all his own, "a quality of song" and "an unfettered diction" that can still make him an inspiration as well as a pleasure. It is not therefore surprising to find Yevtushenko in 1965 invoking Pushkin—as well as Lermontov, Nekrasov, Blok, Pasternak, Yesenin, and Mayakovsky—in his "Invocation Before a Poem" at the start of his long, extraordinary poetic work *The GES at Bratsk*,[9] in which he attempts with varied success to grasp the many-sided aspects of his Mother Russia as she historically is and was.

It is pointless and unrewarding to interfere either "scientifically" or politically with the poet, whose instinct, intuition, and imagination are a better touchstone as to what is best and most fit for the time he lives in, assuming he has an ear for the language and rhythm of his day. But as a modern Russian poet has said, "All the tyrants of Russia have always feared poets as their most dangerous political enemies. They feared Pushkin, then Lermontov, then Nekrasov." Poems of praise and joy have their place if felt and experienced, but they cannot be the poet's only contribution to the age he lives in. In the days of the so-called "cult

---

9. *Yunost*, No. 4, 1965. Literally "The Hydroelectric Station at Bratsk." Bratsk is the site of this gigantic undertaking in Siberia. Three poems from the "Bratsk" cycle are included in the anthology.

of the personality," sycophantic praise of Stalin became obligatory. A pseudoclassical style hedged in by dogmatic requirements and sugared with a tyrant's praise and exaggerated claims is hardly the answer to the challenge of an epoch that is revolutionary in more ways than one. To have condemned, destroyed, and largely frustrated at least three generations of poets, by labeling them "formalist" and "subjective," or even "traitor," as the Stalinists have repeatedly done, is sheer madness and an inexcusable waste of human and national resources. Poets of quality and vision are not so easily come by, and what they have to say is hardly ever immediately obvious. And the artistic tastes of politicians are more often crude and moralistically superficial. Thus a good many poets of "the Silver Age," those born in the 1880's and 1890's, who represented a generation of the highest quality, were needlessly hampered or sacrificed in the years 1918–1953. So were many others who emerged only in the 1920's and 1930's. Others again were lost in the 1940's. One is not likely to forget the Stalinist purges (1936–39), or Zhdanov's brutal assault against the arts in 1946,[10] or the final gathering fury of the anticosmopolitan drive (1948–53), which was directed against "Western influences" and internationally minded Soviet Jews.

The yardstick with which those who were accused of being "formalists" and "subjective" have been drubbed since 1934 (there were other yardsticks before) was that of "Socialist Realism," which has been defined as

the basic method of Soviet literature and literary criticism. It demands of the artist the truthful, historically concrete representation of reality in its revolutionary development. Moreover, the truthfulness and historical concreteness of the artistic representation of reality must be linked with the task of ideological transformation and education of workers in the spirit of socialism.

This statute of the Union of Soviet Writers (that single Union which replaced in 1932 all other groupings of writers) is still on the books. Even though Stalin's death and the subsequent revelations about his duplicity were followed by a crisis of belief and a

---

10. This began on August 14, when a Central Committee resolution condemned the magazines *Zvezda* and *Leningrad*. The poet Anna Akhmatova and the short-story writer Mikhail Zoshchenko were violently attacked and later expelled from the Writer's Union. The attack spread to Pasternak and many other writers and composers.

period of critical re-evaluation, persistent efforts have been made to apply this statute more strictly, particularly in 1956–57, 1959, and in 1962–63. These attempts have brought discomfort or temporary disgrace at various times to a number of writers. But it has been found that certain Soviet poets and novelists are now on the whole more resilient and resistant, and that the statute on Socialist Realism cannot be really made effective without the threat of dire physical compulsion. When applied at gunpoint in 1936 and 1946, it nearly killed off what remained of Russian literature. This now seems unthinkable. Yet the rather arbitrary procedures at the trials of Iosif Brodsky in Leningrad in 1964 and of Andrey Sinyavsky and Yury Daniel in Moscow in 1966 are a sign that coercion against writers can still be exercised.

The dogmatists still exist. They favor the simpler integral solution. They still believe in the "scientific" validity of their utopian prescription and they regard art as merely a secondary, reflected activity—a view of art which the Central Committee had summed up in its Decree of August 14, 1946: "Soviet literature . . . is a literature for which there can be no other interests than those of the people and of the state." But in the post-Stalinist Russia of today such an absolute principle, though it had been restated in a slightly different way by Nikita Khrushchev, is much harder, perhaps impossible, to enforce.

Thus, there are the scientific dogmatists and the dogmatic scientists, who are only too willing to issue prescriptions for or decrees about poetry in the Zhdanov 1946 manner. But, in the Soviet "atomic society" of the 1960's there are also scientists of another sort who are far from being narrowly orthodox. There are now Soviet physicists who enjoy and collect the type of "formalist" painting and poetry which the "dogmatists" abhor and try to suppress by labeling their authors as "the lackeys of bourgeois ideology." Thus, recently, Professor P. L. Kapitza of the Institute of Physical Problems tried to attract attention to an officially neglected painter of talent, a certain Anikeyenok from the Tartar city of Kazan. This artist was accused of not painting according to the "rules" and of being "a frightful example of what can happen to an artist when he departs from the path of Socialist Realism." In this case, however, *Komsomolskaya Pravda* came to the defense of the artist: "His unusual style and search for original forms of expression frighten those who should be helping to direct and support originality and individuality among young people."[11] This Soviet newspaper would therefore seem to support what a young poet had written some ten years ago—"I want art to be as diverse as myself."[12] But in the past ten years the poet has been severely reprimanded many times for daring to show his diversity. That *Komsomolskaya Pravda* has ventured to make its above statement—and we must recall that Sergey Pavlov, the head of the Komsomol, has been up to now one of the most vehement critics of the new poetry and the new art—may very well be due to the fact that the Kazan artist in question was defended by a physicist, i.e., a scientist of repute who is probably held in more respect than a young poet. Indeed, in a poem entitled "Physicists and Lyricists," Boris Slutsky, a poet included in this volume, ironically says as much:

> *Physicists are somehow much in honor;*
> *Lyricists are somehow pushed aside.*

Andrey Voznesensky is another poet who has been particularly concerned with the situation of the poet in an age of automation, robots, and nuclear physics. In his long complex poem "Oza" (1964), he develops a dialogue between a lyrical poet and a physicist whose notebook is found "in a drawer of a night table in a hotel in Dubna." But the poem has also many digressions, such as a satiric piece on the insufferable influence of Stalin—"No more shall we be asphyxiated/in the drooping smoke of his gray hair."—and a parody of Poe's "Raven," where there is a confrontation between a poet's aspirations and delight in life and their vulgar negative:

> *How impress upon him the low cur,*
> *that we're not living here to croak—*
> *but to touch with our lips the wonder*
> *of a kiss or a running stream!*

It may also be remarked that the reactions of the Soviet press these days can sometimes be unexpected. Only a few months ago

11. This incident was reported in the *New York Times* of June 4, 1966.
12. From "Prologue" (1957) in *The Poetry of Yevgeny Yevtushenko*. Ed. and tr. by George Reavey. October House Inc., New York, 1965.

the editor of *Pravda* could be observed advocating in print a more liberal or, let us say, sensible attitude to the arts as against the more orthodox opinions expressed in *Izvestia*. *Pravda* actually printed the statement that "Communist criticism must rid itself of the tone of literary command." This argument is a sign of a healthy diversity of opinion even in official circles. However, in this particular case the author of the above opinion was removed to another post. Thus, whatever the outcome, we are at least made aware of a strenuous tug of war going on in every field of Soviet endeavor, and there is growing alarm that the younger generation has outgrown the stale clichés of the old-type propaganda. And there is the great potential audience for the new poetry, which offers a freshness of language and a novelty of image that had long been lost.

3. THE NEW ATMOSPHERE—POETRY AND IDEOLOGY AFTER 1953

By the "new Russian poets" here, I mean those poets who have helped in the 'fifties or are still helping to create a new atmosphere in Soviet poetry. This atmosphere is compounded of a new outlook on life and the restoration of an abandoned poetic tradition. This restoration involves, above all, the rehabilitation of previously neglected or persecuted poets, such as Nikolai Zabolotzky, Boris Pasternak, Leonid Martynov, and the publication of the works (and commentaries upon them) of those poets of the Silver Age and the 'twenties and 'thirties who were almost entirely eliminated from Soviet letters—poets such as Anna Akhmatova, Osip Mandelshtam, Sergey Yesenin, Marina Tsvetayeva, and Andrey Biely, i.e., those poets who had been thought to be too "subjective," "formalist," or "alien to the Soviet way of life." The new outlook is made up of a new sense of history, awareness of the need for personal responsibility, an acuter critical attitude, and a deeper insight into the emotions of the ordinary man.

Poetically, this outlook consists in a renewed joy in the rich possibilities of language and form, and in a reawakened interest in a more varied subject matter, which does not exclude the inner world of man. All this implies a keener, fresher, more direct scrutiny of the world as well as the exercise of a freer imagination in apprehending the realities and the mysteries of man, society, and the world. The word "mystery" may strike one as provocatively antimaterialistic in the present Soviet context, but modern physics, chemistry, biology, and science as a whole, in contrast to the more limited nineteenth-century realism, are tending to make the universe increasingly mysterious. A number of young Soviet poets have begun to realize this too.

In a brief survey of the Soviet poetry scene today one cannot help but notice a growing excitement and competitive tension in the arena of poetry, which have been missing since the 1920's. But even more than that, poetry today has spilled over from a more restricted habitat into the streets, the public squares, the concert halls, and even the stadiums. The peak was reached when an audience of 14,000 listened to poems being declaimed by young poets in a Moscow stadium in 1962. The authorities became alarmed at this excessive popularity of the free-wheeling versifiers, and some restrictions were imposed upon the more public gatherings such as those in Mayakovsky Square. These public manifesttaions may be said to have begun with the institution of Poetry Day in September, 1955. As a corollary of this celebration, an annual almanac, *Den Poezii* (*The Day of Poetry*), was founded in 1956. Since then the tradition of Poetry Day and *Den Poezii* has spread to Leningrad and other cities as far away as Tbilisi and Alma Ata.

A number of magazines were founded or revived in the middle 'fifties, all of which opened their pages to the poets. Among them were: *Yunost* (1955), *Molodaya Gvardia* (1956), *Moskva* (1957), *Voprosy Literaturi* (1957). A number of almanacs, such as *Literaturnaya Moskva* (1956) and *Taruskiye Stranitzi* (1961), also appeared to enliven the scene. They published selections of poems as well as some of the latest prose and pages devoted to the hitherto neglected poets. Thus *Literaturnaya Moskva II* printed batches of Tsvetayeva's and Zabolotzky's poems. To enliven the scene still further, a series of subterranean mimeographed almanacs—*Syntaksis* I, II, III (1959–60), *Phoenix* I (1961), *Cocktail* (1961), *Sphinxes* (1965)—appeared in limited editions of about 200 copies, each issue containing the work of poets who were not being printed in the established magazines. Some of the underground magazines were seized by the authorities and their editors

arrested. Poems by Okudzhava, Akhmadulina, Brodsky, Kharabarov, and Slutsky have been first presented in this form.

All this varied activity in the domain of poetry indicates the
pressure of a new, restless, and less hidebound generation of
poets, as well as an increasingly alert public not only ready to
respond but eagerly expecting some fresh poetic statement, free
from official jargon, that might throw some light on their doubts
and aspirations after the demise of Stalin. It was the atmosphere
of *The Thaw*, as Ehrenburg called his timely novel, the opposite
of the sort of world Leonid Martynov describes in his poem
"Cold":

> *An experiment was made*
> *To freeze all things—*
> *To cast such grayness*
> *On everything,*
> *So that each town*
> *Might be chained in chill . . .*

Already in the December, 1953, issue of *Novy Mir* (the literary
monthly then, as now, edited by Alexander Tvardovsky) there
appeared an article by V. Pomerantzev in which he argued against
tendentiousness in Soviet literature. Its title "On Sincerity in
Literature" struck what was to become a keynote of the decade
—the new poet or novelist must be sincere and outspoken, no
stooge or hypocrite. Pomerantzev also argued for a greater variety
of theme. Yevtushenko's line, "Then let us be extremely frank,"
pointed in the same direction. Naturally, Pomerantzev was
strongly criticized on all sides, but his plea was supported by some
writers. But this natural and belated trend was immediately
labeled "nihilistic," and the editorial board of *Novy Mir* was
eventually reprimanded by the Praesidium of the Writers' Union
for its "errors" in not opposing "all manifestations of apolitical,
formalistic and non-ideological" activity.

But this measure could not arrest the gradually rising tide of
those who clamored for a broader base and a freer hand for writers.
True, between 1955 and 1957 the authorities tried to put the
brake on again. It was the time of Dudintsev's *Not By Bread
Alone*, Yevtushenko's "Winter Station" (1956), and many other
works which were thought "to distort Soviet reality." It was also

the time of the Twentieth Party Congress (1956) and the Hungarian Revolt, in which writers had played an important part, and general unrest among the satellite Communist parties. As one Soviet literary historian puts it, ". . . never has Socialist ideology experienced such a furious onslaught on the part of its ideological opponents. . . . Revisionists of all sorts tried to exploit the criticism of J. V. Stalin's cult of personality by attacking Communism. . . . In various countries articles appeared directed against Socialist Realism . . . against the Party control of literature. . . ." In official eyes, a section of the Soviet intelligentsia was likewise becoming ideologically affected. The authorities became alarmed, and by 1957 Nikita Khrushchev in person began to intervene and restate the ideological principles that were supposed to guide the development of Soviet literature. But Khrushchev's "secret speech" in 1956 about Stalin's misdeeds only fanned the flames of unrest in the long run. It took five or six years more for poems like Yevtushenko's "Babii Yar" and "The Heirs of Stalin," Tvardovsky's "Tyorkin in the Other World," Ehrenburg's *People, Years, Life*, and Solzhenitsyn's *One Day in the Life of Ivan Denisovich* to appear. It was in this troubled atmosphere that Boris Pasternak published his *Doctor Zhivago* abroad, after failing to get it accepted by the editors of *Novy Mir*.

In general, it may be said that, despite periodical "braking" from on high or the persistent sniping by antagonistic conservative critics, the base for Soviet writing has steadily widened. The controls are still there, but they are usually not applied with the same frightening rigor as they were previously. It is not my intention here to give a minutely detailed account of a decade of closely engaged struggle between the liberal and conservative camps in Soviet literature. To do so would only obscure the positive image of the new poets. Several excellent studies of the ideological aspects already exist, and they may be consulted by anyone wishing to delve further into this bloodthirsty world of verbal throat-slitting.[13]

---

13. *Politics in the Soviet Union. Seven Cases.* Ed. Alexander Dallin and Alan F. Westin. Harcourt Brace & World Inc. N.Y., 1966; Priscilla Johnson. *Krushchev and the Arts.* M.I.T. Press. Cambridge, 1965; *Soviet Literature in the Sixties.* Ed. Max Hayward and Edward L. Crowley. Frederick A. Praeger. N.Y., 1964.

4. THE TIME FOR RE-EVALUATION: DOUBTS AND ASPIRATIONS

Today we are undoubtedly witnessing a revival of Russian poetry. I call it "Russian" advisedly, because "Soviet" is a broader term that also comprises the Union Republics, and I am not in a position at present to judge how far the poetic revival has spread to Uzbekistan or Turkmenia, though it may well be manifesting itself already in Georgia, that Caucasian land of sophisticated poets and wine lovers. One thing may be indicative. The Georgians in Tbilisi have in the recent past published poems by Pasternak, Akhmadulina ("Rain"), and others—poems which were not printed at that time in Moscow.

It is perhaps too early to pass judgment on the quality of the post-1953 poetic revival. To do so, one would have to compare the new poets with the more seasoned veterans of the Silver Age who did part of their work in pre-Revolutionary days. The majority of the new poets are in their twenties, thirties, and forties, and they have started publishing only in the last decade. There are, of course, some older and more established figures among them—Leonid Leonov and Alexander Tvardovsky, for example—whose later work and aspirations seem to fit in better with the post-Stalinist times. But there can be no doubt about the seriousness, talent, and enthusiasm of the new generation of poets. They are not only developing individual themes (though they have some themes in common) and techniques, but some of them are also showing an extraordinary grasp of poetic language and form at the risk of being dubbed "formalists." Courage is another prerequisite in which many of them are not wanting. Without courage it would be difficult to stand up to and maneuver among the ideological pontiffs. Yevtushenko's confrontation with Khrushchev on December 17, 1962, illustrates this point: "The time is long past when only the grave straightens out the hunchbacked."

Kornei Chukovsky, the distinguished author and erstwhile translator of Walt Whitman, some months ago said this about the poetic revival:

For me, there is great personal satisfaction in the fact that poetry is again the leading genre in Russian literature. As in the days of

Alexander Blok and Vladimir Mayakovsky, Russians are seeking and finding in the work of our poets a reflection of their own emotions and beliefs, the foremost of which is a deep hatred of all forms of falsehood. There is a bountiful harvest of talent in our poetry today. I never dreamed I would live to see it in such a great renaissance. . . ."[14]

This statement of Chukovsky's helps to explain the wide impact the new poetry is having in editions of from 50,000 to 150,000 copies, whereas most of Pasternak's editions in the old days never exceeded about 20,000.[15] The Russians, always an emotional people, have gone through enthusiasms, terrors, purges, bloody war, and a final deflation of many ideals including the *reductio ad absurdum* of a hero-father image to the "cult of the personality." In 1962 Stalin's body was removed from the Lenin Mausoleum. Many statues to him were also torn down. It is of this that Alexander Tvardovsky seems to be speaking in his poem "The Statue's Sundered Plinth":

> *The statue's sundered plinth is being smashed,*
> *The steel of drills is sending up a howl.*
> *The special hardset mixture of cement*
> *Was calculated to endure millennia.*
> *The time for re-evaluation came so soon. . . .*

This is no statue of Ozymandias swallowed by desert sands. It is a statue "reduced to scrap by human hands," a symbolic shattering of so much blind faith among those who did not realize the full extent of the corruption and machinations involved in the Leader's ruthless way of running and foreshortening the lives of others.

"Re-evaluation came so soon. . . ." Yes, there was need of it. Need of criticism. Of salutary doubt. Even skepticism. Of irony, the weapon of the unbeliever. Why had so many innocent men and women been butchered, starved? Why should Jews be persecuted in the Soviet Union too? Jewish doctors falsely accused of monstrous plots? Why should poets be driven to suicide? Why should modern art, even impressionism, be considered degen-

---

14. "Visit to Peredelkino." *New York Times* Magazine Section, January 30, 1966, p. 37.
15. The most recent—1966—edition of Pasternak's *Stikhi* (*Verses*), a selection of his poems, numbers 100,000 copies.

erate and made a mock of? Was Socialist Realism a reality? Why should so many lies have been propagated? Why so much sheer hypocrisy? Was the Revolution dead?—These and a host of other disturbing questions assailed not only the young poets but much of the population as well. Doubts there had to be, but not everyone could live by doubt. Purification there had to be. A restoration of belief even if only in a purer language. It was necessary to rediscover some Russian virtues outside of militant puritanism, to rediscover feeling, warmth, compassion. The Russian landscape too. The poet knows what he does not want to be. But he is also determined "to be." Only by being can he do something to repair the damage, to cleanse what is rotten, to make up for deception and betrayal. What can he do? He can at least defend innocence, the integrity of art, expose injustice, inveigh against corruption. Lyricism in itself has a certain quality of innocence. Boris Pasternak's "Hamlet" lyrically confronts the universe and sees himself involved in "a drama of duty and self-denial," a sort of ritual of self-sacrifice to protest the vicious circle of corruption and hypocrisy:

> *I'm alone. The Pharisees swamp all.*
> *Living is no country stroll.*

Andrey Voznesensky, on the other hand, asks in "Oza":

> *Will the trochee, silver flutist, perish*
> *As trout have died when blocked by river dams?*

The voices of those who have suffered blend with the voices of those who still have hope. Therein lies the essential drama and the rekindling power of the new Russian poetry as it struggles to rise to new human heights above the welter of conflict and falsehood, and above "the daily grind" against which Mayakovsky's "boat of love" had crashed, and renew itself in the purer "running stream" of lyrical energy.

5. THE INDIVIDUAL POETS. THEIR STYLE AND THEME

It is clear at a glance that the new poets use a variety of forms. It is certainly not any particular poetic form that unites or distinguishes them from their immediate predecessors. They are freer to experiment with form and to use various combinations. The two extremes are, perhaps, to be found in Bella Akhumadulina and Andrey Voznesensky. Akhmadulina has tended on the sur-́ face to keep to the pattern of classical rhymed stanzas, but her meter is more subtle and broken than would appear at first sight. But in her longer poem "My Genealogy" we also find her using more varied forms. Voznesensky, on the other hand, has moved very rapidly from the comparative simplicity of his earlier lyrics to an increasingly complex form of presentation. He was complex enough in his "Digressions," but in "Oza" he went a step further from the standpoint of form, producing a hybrid of alternating passages of verse and prose. His verse, already varied enough, now ranges from simple narrative and love song to philosophical comment, parody and satire. His verbal texture is tricky; he is fond of manipulating verbal roots and using a great deal of assonance and alliteration. Victor Sosnora of Leningrad, a poet of smaller range, to date, is another who manages to create a sort of impasto of verbal effects that reminds one of the language-delving and language-recreation once carried on by Victor Khlebnikov (1885–1922), officially a Russian Futurist, but in reality a deeply Slavic, fanatic lover of the word, a sort of wilder, stranger Gerard Manley Hopkins. In some of his earlier poems, Ivan Kharabarov also has some of the same dense textural verbal quality and, in form, there is some similarity between him and Sosnora.

In Leonid Martynov and Yevgeny Vinokurov we see two poets of different generations, who yet have some affinity in their simplicity of language and clarity of form, as well as in their attitude of restrained commentators upon life and history. They both also tend to be somewhat abstract. Yet there are essential differences. Martynov, who suffered from repression in the Stalinist era and who wrote many poems without being able to publish them, emerged in 1956 with his *Verses*, which then had considerable repercussions. His later poems, though still restrained in tone, are much freer in form, but his lines are meticulously and economically architectured. In simple but carefully chosen words he makes almost wry but still lyrical comments on various aspects of life including those which are of the greatest concern to all thinking Russians. His work has increased in popularity and he has exercised a considerable influence on the younger poets. Vinokurov, a war veteran, is also steadily attracting an ever wider audience. His comments on life are distinctly more philosophical, even metaphysical, yet he manages to combine his philosophy with a concrete sense of everyday life. From being mainly concerned with his war experiences, like so many others, he is becoming increasingly interested in people or "characters." His form might be called spontaneous and transparent. One is hardly aware of it. His vocabulary, again, is simple. One is never arrested by any strange combination of words or syllables. There is no rich texture and seldom a striking image; and yet a song comes through and, with it, the image of a situation and, beyond it, a question is raised. In Stalin's time, his poetry might have been condemned as "idealist," as was Pasternak's esthetic and autobiographical essay, *Safe Conduct*, in 1931.

Victor Bokov, another victim of the past, has turned out to be a very natural and pure lyricist of deeply Russian feeling and language. He is no modernist and does not pursue form for its own sake. His domain is the countryside; nature, his companion. He is essentially a nature poet, though he also writes of love and war. He is personally much appreciated by poets like Voznesensky and Yevtushenko.

Novella Matveyeva, the second woman poet to be included in this anthology, is very different, both in the form and content of her poetry, from Bella Akhmadulina. She lacks the latter's classic polish, sense of irony, and lyrical coolness. She tends to write rather longer lyrics in a somewhat freer form. She plunges into and gets wrapped up in her subject. Her language is denser and she likes using lyrical refrains which are also images. Her world is a childhood world, a world of dreams, memories, and quick impressions. In her dream-like "Hypnosis," however, she shows herself capable of writing a long sustained poem of meticulously elegant description of a tropical scene, which brings to mind a Douanier Rousseau landscape.

To read Bulat Okudzhava is to experience a warm, friendly feeling. Here is a poet, who has been through the hell of war and still loves life and song. He sings of love and ordinary people. He also sings of war, but not to glorify it as his "Paper Soldier" will demonstrate. He is outspoken and sincere. He has a sense of varied rhythm, and his form is plastic and adaptable.

Robert Rozhdestvensky, one of the pioneers of the middle 1950's, has done much traveling in the Soviet Union, and this is reflected in his various cycles of poems. He writes of love and travel, and occasionally touches upon civic issues. His poems tend to be long, because he splits the lines into word and phrase patterns, a style of writing developed by Mayakovsky and Asseyev. He has been severely criticized in the past, but is perhaps today not the pioneer he used to be. Yevgeny Yevtushenko is undoubtedly the best known of the younger poets of this decade. He is the only one of them to have written and published an extremely interesting and revealing *Autobiography*. He is a poet of great energy, courage, and extreme determination. His poetic work is growing by leaps and bounds. As a poet, he combines a strain of personal, more intimate lyricism with what he feels to be his civic mission of exposing and castigating those who foster injustice or hide corruption. He can be a Hamlet-gladiator in the Coliseum in Rome or he can argue with Khrushchev and roundly tell off the leader of the Komsomol ("Letter to Yesenin"). His form is varied; his texture thinner or richer. His content can be appealing or provoking. He can not only be a militant tribune, but also a moody lyricist as in his recent poem "The Sigh"[16]:

> And now I'm tired.
> > I've become shut in,
> I have ceased to trust.
> At times, when in my cups,
> I almost catch myself exploding.
> But no explosion comes,
> > only a sigh . . .

Iosif Brodsky is perhaps the strangest and most isolated of the poets. In a sense, everything is still ahead for him. By some he is considered the most promising of Soviet poets. He certainly has rich technique for one so young. It is to be hoped that he will soon be released from his banishment. He is a poet of strange imagination. Both his city and his countryside are ghostly. His feeling of loneliness is alarming. And yet his rich and peculiar talent must be allowed to flourish.

---

16. *Den Poezii*. M. 1965

Iosif Brodsky is certainly an exception on the Soviet scene. So, in another way, is Yury Galanskov, whose formally Mayakovskian "The Human Manifesto" is outwardly the most rebellious poem in this collection. The poem is hardly typical of other Soviet work, and could only have been published in one of the "underground" magazines—in this case *Phoenix* I. Leonid Gubanov, the youngest of all, is just beginning to publish. In his latest poems he seems to be influenced by Khlebnikov. He has already been in trouble. It is to be hoped he has a strong backbone.

The themes most of these poets have in common are the memories of war and suffering, Russian nature, a sense of compassion for the ordinary man, a renewal of the love theme, hatred of falsehood and corruption, a desire to find a new justification and ideal for the Revolution, and the need to insist on the integrity of the artist.

In an Anthology such as this, which suffers from the limitations imposed upon it by the bilingual texts, it has been impossible to include a number of other new poets of interest and quality (Yuna Moritz, Naum Korzhavin, Vladimir Tsybin, David Samoilov, Tamara Zhirmuskaya, Rimma Kozakova, and certain others, for example). This omission may later be repaired.

GEORGE REAVEY
New York, May, 1966

THE NEW RUSSIAN POETS: 1953 to 1966

BORIS PASTERNAK

1890–1960

As a poet, Boris Pasternak can be seen in the light of at least four rather distinct periods. His first period (1912–23) culminated in the twin volumes *My Sister Life* and *Themes and Variations*. In his second period (1923–32), Pasternak attempted to grapple with the Russian Revolution as an historical event (in his *1905*, *Captain Schmidt* and *The Waves*). The third period (1932–53), that of *On Early Trains* and *Spacious Earth*, a period also full of silences, consisted of his attempt to resolve in his own way the problems arising out of the Stalinist insistence on the platform of Socialist Realism. This was the period of collectivization, the purges, the war, the Zhdanov restrictions and the drive against cosmopolitanism. For all its terrors, this protracted period of apparent frustration but intense inner concentration laid the foundation for Pasternak's ultimate international fame (the *Doctor Zhivago* novel and the Nobel Prize 1958). But Pasternak also produced new cycles of poems (the *Zhivago* and the *Rift In The Cloud* cycles), which were different in theme, tone and technique from his earlier work. Thus, as from 1954, Pasternak re-emerges in a new light as an influential poet of the Fifties. This is what justifies his inclusion in this anthology of New Poets. The intensely dramatic "Hamlet" poem illustrates not only his new theme and style, but also his impact on the younger generation—the poem was included in one of the "underground" magazines in 1961. The second poem, "Insomnia" (1953) was published posthumously and shows that the full extent of Pasternak's later work is not yet known.—Pasternak was born in Moscow. His father was a distinguished portraitist and illustrator. By 1912, Boris Pasternak had decided to be a poet after exploring the possibilities of music and philosophy. He was to prove an essentially lyrical poet. His later poetic development was considerably delayed owing to the mistaken zeal of the dogmatist critics.

ГАМЛЕТ

Гул затих. Я вышел на подмостки.
Прислонясь к дверному косяку,
Я ловлю в далеком отголоске
Что случилось на моем веку.

На меня наставлен сумрак ночи
Тысячью биноклей на оси.
Если только можно, абба отче,
Чашу эту мимо пронеси.

Я люблю твой замысел упрямый
И играть согласен эту роль.
Но сейчас идет другая драма,
И на этот раз меня уволь.

Но продуман распорядок действий,
И неотвратим конец пути.
Я, один, все тонет в фарисействе.
Жизнь прожить — не поле перейти.

БЕССОННИЦА

Который час? Темно. Наверно, — третий.
Опять мне, видно, глаз сомкнуть не суждено.
Пастух в поселке щелкнет плетью на рассвете.
Потянет холодом в окно,
Которое во двор обращено.
А я один.
Неправда, ты
Всей белизны своей сквозной волной
Со мной.

HAMLET

Talk is hushed. I tread the boards.
Leaning on the post of the door,
Distantly I catch the stir
Of what's happening in this age.

Darkly night admonishes
With a thousand lenses trained.
Abba Father, if Thou wouldst,
Bear this chalice past my lips.

I adore Thy strict design,
And consent to act this part.
But another drama's playing:
So, for once, may I be spared.

But the acts have been ordained,
Irreversible the journey's end.
I'm alone. The Pharisees swamp all.
Living is no country stroll.

1954

INSOMNIA

What time is it? It's dark. Getting on to three.
Again, apparently, I'm not to close my eyes.
The village herdsman will crack his whip at dawn.
Cold air will blow in at the window
Which overlooks the yard.
And I'm alone.
Not true. With all
The penetrating wave of your white self
You're here with me.

1953 (1965)

ALEXANDER TVARDOVSKY

1910–

Alexander Tvardovsky is both a leading poet and a famous editor. For some years he has been chief editor of *Novy Mir* which is, perhaps, the best known Soviet literary magazine. Though a poet of an older generation, who made his literary debut in the middle 1930's and who consolidated his reputation during the war with a long narrative poem, *Vasily Tyorkin* (1942), Tvardovsky has become increasingly important as a poet and editor in the last ten years. As a poet, Tvardovsky has been concerned with "re-evaluation" in the post-Stalinist period. This is very clear from his bold satirical and narrative poem, *Vasily Tyorkin In The Other World* (1963) and his latest meditative lyrical cycle of "New Poems" (1963–65). As an editor, Tvardovsky has played a very important part in encouraging new and controversial talent, as his publication of Solzhenitsyn's *One Day* so clearly demonstrates.

Alexander Tvardovsky was born in the Smolensk region, the son of a blacksmith. He began to write verse at an early age. He published his first poems in the local papers. In Moscow he was first printed in *Oktyabr*. But he continued living in Smolensk where he took courses in higher education. In 1935 he moved to Moscow, and his literary career may be said to date from then.

Дробится рваный цоколь монумента,
Взвывает сталь отбойных молотков.
Крутой раствор особого цемента
Рассчитан был на тысячи веков.
Пришло так быстро время пересчета,
И так нагляден нынешний урок:
Чрезмерная о вечности забота —
Она, по справедливости, не впрок.
Но как сцепились намертво каменья,
Разъять их силой — выдать семь потов.
Чрезмерная забота о забвенье
Немалых тоже требует трудов.
Все, что на свете сделано руками,
Рукам под силу обратить на слом.
Но дело в том,
Что сам собою камень, —
Он не бывает ни добром, ни злом.

THE STATUE'S SUNDERED PLINTH

The statue's sundered plinth is being smashed,
The steel of drills is sending up a howl.
The special hardset mixture of cement
Was calculated to endure millennia.
The time for re-evaluation came so soon.
And the present lesson is quite obvious:
Excessive concentration on eternity
Brings no advantage, we can justly say.
But these strong stones have such a deadly hold,
We have to sweat to force them break apart.
Excessive concentration on oblivion
Requires no small amount of labor too.
All handmade things in the world we live in
Can be reduced to scrap by hands of men.
But the main point is this:
Stone in its essence can
Be never either good or bad.

From "New Poems 1963–65"

LEONID MARTYNOV

1905–

Another poet of an older generation, Leonid Martynov only began to come into his own after the demise of Stalin. His poetic career seems to fall into two very distinct parts: as from 1939 to 1945, when he published three books; and as from 1955 when he becomes increasingly prominent, publishing widely in magazines and in book form. He is essentially a lyrical poet of keen observation and precision, preferring the use of simple words and colloquial turns of speech. In some ways he might be compared to William Carlos Williams. He is much respected by the younger generation of poets and has, since the publication of his *Stikhi* (1956), exercised a considerable influence on them.

Leonid Martynov was born in Omsk, Siberia. His father was a State employee. As from 1921, he began to work on newspapers and, to begin with, on the Omsk *Rabochii Put*. It was in Omsk that Martynov published his first volume, *Verses and Poems* (1939). For the past twenty years he has been living in Moscow. Many of his poems of the 1940's, which he could not publish at the time, have only recently been included in his later volumes.

Мне кажется, что я воскрес.
Я жил. Я звался Геркулес.
Три тысячи пудов я весил.
С корнями вырывал я лес.
Рукой тянулся до небес.
Садясь, ломал я спинки кресел.
И умер я... И вот воскрес:
Нормальный рост, нормальный вес —
Я стал как все. Я добр, я весел.
Я не ломаю спинки кресел...
И все-таки я Геркулес.

HERCULES

It seems I have been resurrected.
I lived before. And my name was Hercules.
I weighed a hundred tons.
I tore up a forest by the roots.
With my hand I grasped at the skies.
Sitting down, I broke the backs of chairs.
And then I died . . . I've been resurrected since:
of normal stature, normal weight—
I've become like other men. I'm cheerful, kind.
I do not break the backs of chairs,
And, nevertheless, I'm Hercules.

1957

И снова
В небе
Вьются птицы:
Синицы,
Голуби,
Стрижи...

Но есть же все-таки границы,
Пределы, точки, рубежи!

Эй, вы!
Бессмысленно не вейтесь!
Равняйтесь там к плечу плечо,
На треугольники разбейтесь,
Составьте что-нибудь еще!

Но все же
Мечутся,
Виляют
И суматоху развели,
Как будто бы не управляет
Никто решительно с земли.

Неутешительно!
Печально!
Выходит, что управы нет.
Летают, как первоначально —
Тому назад сто тысяч лет!

Довольно!
Я сказал: вмешаюсь!
По радио я прикажу.

BIRDS IN THE SKY

And once again
birds hover
in the sky:
tomtits,
pigeons,
martins . . .

But there are frontiers all the same,
borders, check points, lines of demarcation.

Ah, you birds!
Don't flit so aimlessly there!
Fall in, shoulder to shoulder,
form triangles,
try other formations.

But nevertheless
they dart
and wheel
and cause confusion.
No one on the earth
seems to direct them with authority.

Hardly comforting!
Very sad!
Turns out there's no control.
They fly about as in primordial days
some hundred thousand years ago!

Enough of that!
I must intervene, I said.
I'll issue commands by radio.

И все ж
Вмешаться не решаюсь;
Остановился
И гляжу!

ЛИСТЬЯ

Они
Лежали
На панели.

И вдруг
Они осатанели
И, изменив свою окраску,
Пустились в пляску, колдовские.

Я закричал:
— Вы кто такие?

— Мы — листья,
Листья, листья, листья! —
Они в ответ зашелестели.
— Мечтали мы о пейзажисте,
Но руки, что держали кисти,
Нас полюбить не захотели.
Мы улетели,
Улетели!

And nevertheless
I hesitate to intervene;
stopping,
all I do is stare!

1957

LEAVES

They
Lay
On the footpath

Then suddenly
They were possessed
And, changing their hues,
Began to dance like witches.

"Who are you?"
I yelled.

"We are leaves,
Leaves, leaves, leaves!—"
They rustled in reply,
"We were dreaming of a landscape painter,
But the hand that held the brush
Did not want to love us.
We flew away,
Flew away!"

1957

ЛЮБОВЬ

Ты жива,
Ты жива!
Не сожгли тебя пламень и лава,
Не засыпало пеплом, а только задело едва.
Ты жива,
Как трава,
Увядать не имевшая права;
Будешь ты и в снегах
Зелена и поздней покрова.

И еще над могилой моей
Ты взойдешь, как посмертная слава.
И не будет меня —
Ты останешься вечно жива.
Говори не слова,
А в ответ лишь кивай величаво —
Улыбнись и кивни,
Чтоб замолкла пустая молва.

Ты жива,
Ты права,
Ты отрада моя и отрава,
Каждый час на земле —
Это час твоего торжества!

LOVE

You're alive,
You're alive!
Neither flame, nor lava, have burned you;
Ash has not buried you, barely touching.
You're alive,
Like the grass
That had no right to fade;
Even under the deep snows you'll stay
Green, even after my burial.

And you will rise
Above my grave like posthumous fame.
And even when I am gone,
You will remain living forever.
Speak no word,
Just nod graciously in reply;
Smile and nod,
And quiet all groundless rumor.

You're alive,
You are right,
You are my joy and toxin.
Each hour on earth
Is the hour of your triumph!

ХОЛОД

Был
Создан
Холод.

Был оделан опыт
Все заморозить —
На все набросить
Такую проседь,
Чтоб каждый город
Был стужей скован
И был бы каждый шаг рискован,
И стал бы рваться
Каждый провод,
Чтоб столковаться
Лопнул повод
И замерзал бы каждый довод,
И даже шепот
Мерз бы в горле,
Чтоб вымерзло до основанья
Все: и голубок воркованье
И в ясном небе
Касаток щебет...

Такой был опыт.
Но этот опыт —
Весьма понятно — вызвал ропот...
И лед расколот.

И по теплу и свету голод
Объял весь мир:
Моря, и сушу,
И человеческую
Душу.

COLD

Cold
Was
Created.

An experiment was made
To freeze all things—
To cast such grayness
On everything,
So that each town
Might be chained in chill,
And each step be a risk,
And each cable
Start to break;
So that cause for agreement
Might burst,
And each conclusion be frozen,
And that even a whisper
Freeze in the throat;
So that, to its foundations,
All things might congeal: even the cooing of doves
And, in the clear sky,
The twittering of swallows . . .

Such the experiment.
But this experiment—
Quite understandably—roused discontent . . .
And the ice was broken.

And a hungering for warmth and light
Enfolded the whole world:
The seas and the dry land,
And the human
Soul.

1961

Еще
Боятся
Высоты:
Мол, с высоты легко сорваться
И ввысь уж лучше не соваться...

Еще
Боятся простоты:
Мол, попросту не столковаться.

Еще
Боятся
Наготы,
Хоть фиговые листы
Смешны, чтоб ими прикрываться.

Еще
Боятся
Красоты,
Боятся с ней соприкасаться:
Мол, очень трудно разобраться,
Как будто бы в глазах двоятся
Ее блестящие черты.

Отсюда — бденья и посты.

О ты,
Простак,
Пойми же ты:
Ты в рубище лженищеты
За крохами встаешь в хвосты,
Когда кругом твои богатства,
Твои сокровища таятся,
Твои труды,
Твои мечты.

THEY STILL FEAR

They still
Fear
The heights:
It's easy to fall from a height, they say,
And better not climb so high . . .

They still
Fear simplicity:
Simply, they say, you can't agree.

They still
Fear
Nakedness,
Though fig leaves
Make a comic covering.

They still
Fear
Beauty,
Fear its contact:
It's hard to know, they say,
As though beauty's radiant features
Looked double to the eyes.

Hence—they keep vigils and fast.

O simpleton
You,
Please try and understand:
In the rags and tatters of would-be poverty,
You line up for crumbs,
When all around your riches,
Your treasures, lie hidden,
Your works,
Your dreams.

1961

В СТРАНЕ, ГДЕ ЗЕМЛЮ ВЗРЫЛИ ТАНКИ

В стране,
Где землю взрыли танки,
Стоит цветок в консервной банке
На алтаре перед Мадонной
Внутри капеллы разоренной.

Цветок
С головкою склоненной,
Торчит он из консервной банки,
Из опорожненной жестянки,
В которой был напиток детский.

И благосклонно, по-соседски,
В жестянку дождевой водицы
Вливает сумрачное небо
Через разрушенную крышу,
И в зеркальце воды глядится
Мадонна, Пресвятая Дева,
Полуукрывшаяся в нишу,
Сама подобна иностранке
В стране,
Где землю взрыли танки.

IN THE LAND WHERE TANKS

In the land
Where tanks had plowed the soil,
A little flower stands in a can
On the altar in front of the Madonna
Inside a ruined chapel.

The little flower
With head bowed down
Sticks up out of the can,
Out of an emptied can
That once held baby food.

And through the damaged roof
The clouded sky, like a good neighbor,
Benevolently pours
Rainwater into the can.
And in a mirror of water
The Holy Virgin contemplates herself.
Half hidden in a niche,
Resembling a foreigner herself,
In the land
Where tanks had plowed the soil.

1964

НА БЕРЕГУ

На берегу
Я человека встретил,
На берегу морском,
На берегу, где ветер так и метил
Глаза мои запорошить песком,
На берегу, где хмурая собака
Меня обнюхала, а с вышины,
За мной следя, таращился из мрака
Своими кратерами шар луны,
И фонари торчали, как на страже,
Передо мною тень мою гоня.

А человек не оглянулся даже,
Как будто не заметил он меня.
И я ему был очень благодарен,
Воистину была мне дорога
Его рассеянность. Ведь я не барин,
И он мне тоже вовсе не слуга,
И нечего, тревожась и тревожа,
Друг дружку щупать с ног до головы.
Хоть и диктует разум наш, что все же
Еще полезна бдительность, увы!

ON THE SHORE

On the shore
I met a man,
On the seashore,
On the shore where the wind was resolved
To throw sand in my eyes,
On the shore where a sulking dog
Had sniffed me over, while spying
On me from on high, the moon's sphere
With its craters stared out of the dark,
And lanterns jutted forward as if on guard,
Chasing my shadow ahead of me.

And the man did not even glance back
As though he had not even noticed me.
And I was very grateful to him,
And his absent-mindedness
Was truly precious to me. For I'm no lord,
And he, in no way, my servant,
And there's no cause, troubling and being troubled,
To feel each other out from head to foot,
Even if our reason dictates
That vigilance is still, alas, appropriate!

1965

ГИБЕЛЬ МИРА

И когда
Я решил
Этот мир погубить,
Ничего я не стал ни ломать, ни рубить
И не стал выносить приговоры к смертям.

Нет,
Я все эти старые средства отверг —
Крикнул Солнцу: «Ни с места!»,
Земле: «Руки вверх!»

Лишь
На миг
Этот мир
В неподвижность я вверг,
И немедленно все поскакало с орбит,
По инерции все полетело к чертям!

THE DESTRUCTION OF THE WORLD

And when
I resolved
To destroy the world,
I did not begin by smashing or slashing a thing,
And by executing sentences of death.

No,
I rejected all these old means—
I cried out to the sun: "Don't move!"
To the earth: "Hands up!"

For an instant
Only
I plunged
This world into immobility
And all things at once leapt out of orbit;
From sheer inertia all things fell apart!

1965

VICTOR BOKOV

1914–

Victor Bokov can also claim to be a poet of the 1950's, since it was only in 1956 that he began to get printed in the literary magazines. His first book of poems, *Steep-Intoxication*, came out in 1958. He is above all a lyrical poet of the countryside—a sort of softer-spoken Yesenin without any tragic undertones. His poetry, though simpler and less avant-garde than that of his younger contemporaries, is appreciated by poets like Vosnesensky and Yevtushenko, who have dedicated some of their poems to him.

Victor Bokov was born of a peasant family in the village of Yazvitza (Zagorsk, Moscow province). On leaving school, he first worked as a lathe turner in a metal factory. He continued to study in the evenings and, in 1934–38, attended the Gorky Literary Institute in Moscow. Then, till 1942, he worked on a newspaper. Thereafter he joined up and went to the front. After the war he worked as a technician in a State Collective Farm in the Kemerovsk region.

In 1948, he returned to Moscow as a poetry consultant to the All-Union House of Folk Culture. He traveled much, collecting folk songs, *chastushki* and studying folk music. He himself had written poetry since childhood. Mikhail Prishvin was the first to notice his poetic talent. Bokov had also made a study of the *Kalevala*, which he has translated. After 1950 Bokov concentrated on writing songs. His literary reputation dates from 1956, since when he has published a great deal. Previous to that, he also had suffered under the Stalinist regime.

Я люблю твои глаголы:
«не приду», «не жди», «не плачь».
Я люблю твои ладони,
Принимающие мяч.

Я люблю, как ты смеешься!
Губы настежь — снег во рту.
Как ты вдруг играть берешься
В волейбол или лапту.

Я люблю сверканье пяток,
Твой мальчишеский галоп,
Своевольный ветер прядок,
Ниспадающих на лоб.

Я тобой владеть не буду
Ни по лету, ни к зиме.
Только б ты была повсюду,
Только б пела на корме.

I LOVE THE VERBS YOU USE

I love the verbs you use:
"I won't come," "Don't wait," "Don't cry."
I love the palms of your hands
When you are catching a ball.

I love the way you laugh!
Lips wide open—mouth full of snow.
The way you suddenly start playing
At rounders or volleyball.

I love your flashing heels,
The boyish way you gallop.
The wilful wind of your curls
Falling down upon your forehead.

I don't intend to possess you
In summer or at approach of winter.
If only you were everywhere,
Were only singing at the stern.

1958

Разливы рек,
Раскаты грома,
Дождя веселые шаги.
Чего же мне еще? Я — дома,
А дом мой — плащ и сапоги.

И не беда, что сверху мочит,
Литою дробью в спину бьет.
Вот только так душа и хочет,
Уюта лучшего не ждет!

МУЗЫКА

Музыка — как небо над землей.
Все в ней есть: восход, закат, сиянье
И нерасторжимое слиянье
Млечного Пути над головой.

Я, как в небо, в музыку лечу.
Мой корабль — восторженность и трепет.
Музыка меня, как скульптор, лепит,
Я в блаженстве слиться с ней хочу.

Безразлично — скрипка иль орган,
Балалайка, арфа или домра,
Только бы она, моя мадонна,
Музыка! И только б не уран!

THE RIVERS ALL IN FLOOD

The rivers all in flood,
The peals of thunder.
The joyous steps of the rain.
What more do I want? I'm at home.
Boots and a raincoat are my house.

Nothing wrong for rain to drench,
To beat my back with leaden shot.
That's the way the soul would have it;
It expects no better comfort.

1958

MUSIC

Music's like the sky above the earth.
All is there: sunrise, sunset, the glow
And the indissoluble confluence
Of the Milky Way above our head.

I fly into music as into the sky.
The thrill and rapture are my ship.
Music molds me like a sculptor.
Blissfully I wish to blend with it.

An organ or a violin—it doesn't matter,
A balalaika, dombra, or a harp,
Only let it be music,
My Madonna. And not uranium at all!

1965

BORIS SLUTSKY

1919–

Boris Slutsky's first book of poems appeared in 1957. Its title was *Memory*. Since then and up to 1965, he has published three further books. A certain almost crude directness and economy of means are the characteristic of this poet who sees his function as a "telegraph wire" which carries messages in Morse about "events." Slutsky avoids poetic embellishments and ornaments, as well as the sort of play of words that attract some of the younger poets like Voznesensky and Sosnora. Thus he hits straight from the shoulder and insists on "sense." Though not in the vanguard of "modernism," Slutsky's dry and laconic poetic comments have an interest of their own.

Boris Slutsky was born in Slavyansk in the Ukraine. He finished his schooling in Kharkov. From 1937 to 1941 he studied at the Moscow Institute of Jurisprudence and at the same time attended the Gorky Literary Institute. He began to get published in 1941, but, in June, volunteered to go to the front. In 1948–52 he worked at the All-Union Radio.

МОИ ТОВАРИЩИ

Сгорели в танках мои товарищи
до пепла, до золы, дотла.
Трава, полмира покрывающая,
из них, конечно, произросла.
Мои товарищи
                на минах
подорвались,
                взлетели ввысь,
и много звезд, далеких, мирных,
из них,
        моих друзей,
                зажглись.
Про них рассказывают в праздники,
показывают их в кино,
и однокурсники и одноклассники
стихами стали уже давно.

MY COMRADES

They were burnt in tanks, my comrades,
burnt to embers, cinders, reduced to ash.
Grass grew out of them, of course,
grass that spreads over half the world.
My comrades
              were blown up
on mines,
         pitched high in the air,
and many stars, remote and peaceful,
were kindled
        from them,
               from my friends.
There's talk of them on holidays,
they're shown on films,
and those who were my schoolmates and fellow students
have long since become lines in poems.

ФИЗИКИ И ЛИРИКИ

Что-то физики в почете.
Что-то лирики в загоне.
Дело не в сухом расчете,
Дело в мировом законе.
Значит, что-то не раскрыли
Мы, что следовало нам бы!
Значит, слабенькие крылья —
Наши сладенькие ямбы,
И в пегасовом полете
Не взлетают наши кони...
То-то физики в почете,
То-то лирики в загоне.

Это самоочевидно.
Спорить просто бесполезно.
Так что даже не обидно.
А скорее интересно
Наблюдать, как, словно пена,
Опадают наши рифмы
И величие степенно
Отступает в логарифмы.

PHYSICISTS AND LYRICISTS

Physicists are somehow much in honor;
Lyricists are somehow pushed aside.
It's not a question of cold calculation;
It's just a question of universal law.
It seems we've failed to find out what
We should have discovered long ago!
It seems our wings are rather weak—
Weak our mellifluous iambics!
And our steeds do not take off
And soar like Pegasi . . .
That's why physicists are held in honor;
That's why lyricists are pushed aside.

This is self-evident.
It's simply useless to dispute it.
It doesn't even hurt us.
And it is more interesting
To observe how, like foam,
Our rhymes keep flopping down,
And how soberly greatness retreats
Into the world of logarithms.

Гробница Данте. Сюда мы входим
тихо и важно в темпе анданте.
Причин для этого не находим,
но понимаем: Данте — Данте...

Данте — Данте, а мы — не боле
как только мы. Вот граница.
Зависти не испытав и боли,
входим, шапки сломав, в гробницу.

Да, Данте. Он — уже остался,
а мы, знаменитые по два, по три
года,
жребий, что нам достался,
не смеем даже бросить подле.

Покуда гиды вкусно, длительно
рассказывают о его судьбе,
себялюбиво и неуважительно
к себе
            мы думаем о себе.

На дне души, на самом донце,
вдруг отражается светило:
внезапным блеском блещет солнце,
которое ему светило.

DANTE'S TOMB

Dante's tomb. Quietly and solemnly
we enter here—*tempo andante.*
We can't well explain it,
but we understand: Dante . . . Dante . . .

Dante—Dante, and yet we are no more
than what we are. There's a frontier here.
Feeling no envy, pain, we enter
the tomb, crumpling our caps.

Yes, Dante. He has remained,
and we, whose fame lasts two, three
years,
dare not throw down in his vicinity
the lots we drew.

While the guides with gusto
tell us at long length about his fate,
we think of ourselves
with vanity
               and disrespect.

In the very depths of our being,
the luminary glows of a sudden:
the sun shines out in unexpected splendor,
the sun which was his guiding light.

1964

ЛОШАДИ В ОКЕАНЕ

И. Эренбургу

Лошади умеют плавать,
Но — не хорошо. Недалеко.
«Глория» — по-русски значит «Слава», —
Это вам запомнится легко.
Шел корабль, своим названьем гордый.
Океан старался превозмочь.
В трюме, добрыми мотая мордами,
Тыща лошадей топталась день и ночь.
Тыща лошадей! Подков четыре тыщи!
Счастья все ж они не принесли.
Мина кораблю пробила днище
Далеко-далёко от земли.
Люди сели в лодки, в шлюпки влезли.
Лошади поплыли просто так.
Как же быть и что же делать, если
Нету мест на лодках и плотах?
Плыл по океану рыжий остров.
В море, в синем, остров плыл гнедой.
И сперва казалось — плавать просто.
Океан казался им рекой.
Но не видно у реки той края.
На исходе лошадиных сил
Вдруг заржали кони, возражая
Тем, кто в океане их топил.
Кони шли на дно и ржали, ржали,
Все на дно покуда не пошли.
Вот и все. А все-таки мне жаль их,
Рыжих, не увидевших земли.

HORSES IN THE OCEAN

TO ILYA EHRENBURG

Horses know how to swim,
But not so well. Not too far.
In Russian, *"Gloria"* means *"Slava."*
That you can easily remember.
The ship sailed on, proud of its name.
The ocean tried to get the better of it.
In the hold, shaking their good heads,
A thousand horses trampled day and night.
A thousand horses! Four thousand hooves!
All the same they brought no luck,
A mine ripped out the bottom of the ship
when it was a long way from the shore.
The men piled into boats and sloops.
The horses could only swim.
What else could they do when there was no room
For them in the boats and on the rafts?
An island of bays was swimming in the ocean.
In the sea, the blue sea, swam an island of grays.
To swim seemed simple in the beginning.
To them the ocean seemed a river.
But it was a river that had no bank in sight.
When their equine strength was failing,
The horses suddenly began to neigh, protesting
Against those who were drowning them in the ocean.
The horses sank to the bottom, neighing, neighing.
Until they had all gone down.
That is all. Nevertheless, I pity them,
Those bay horses, that never saw the land again.

1965

YEVGENY VINOKUROV

1925–

Yevgeny Vinokurov is another poet whose work only begins to develop in the post-Stalinist era and to assume increasing importance in the Sixties. Beginning with poems of situation and realistic description he has gradually come to write poems of psychological and philosophical implication. In his earlier poems he had been much concerned with digesting and expressing his war experiences. Of late he has increasingly turned to exploring "characters" as his poem "I" would indicate. In style, he is no modernist. He does not play with form or words, and is more interested in facing the "obvious" and imparting to it a certain depth of philosophical meaning. His choice of words, in contrast with Voznesensky for example, is "ordinary." His philosophical bent is, however, rather unusual in Soviet poetry to date.

Yevgeny Vinokurov was born in Bryansk. His father was a State employee. In World War II Vinokurov fought as a paratrooper. In 1947 he began studying geology, but a year later joined the Gorky Literary Institute where he completed his courses in 1951. He began to appear in print in 1948. His first book of poems, *Poems About Duty*, came out in 1951 and his second in 1956. Since then he has published some ten books, six of them between 1960 and 1965.

НЕЗАБУДКИ

В шинельке драной, без обуток
Я помню в поле мертвеца.
Толпа кровавых незабудок
Стояла около лица.

Мертвец лежал недвижно, глядя,
Как медлил коршун вдалеке.
И было выколото «Надя»
На обескровленной руке...

И в мире, где все граница,
Все только предел и преграда,
Бездонная бесконечность,—
Ты мне лишь одна отрада!
...Какая-то в щели сарая
Синеющая полоска —
И вот уж свидетельство: в мире
Не все уж так просто и плоско!

FORGET-ME-NOTS

In a ragged soldier's coat, without boots,
The dead man, I recall, was lying in a field.
A crowd of blood-stained forget-me-nots
Stood near his face.

The dead man lay motionless, his gaze
On a vulture hovering at a distance.
And Nadya—a girl's name,
Was tattooed on his bloodless hand . . .

AND IN A WORLD

And in a world, where all is frontier,
All merely boundary and barrier,
You are, fathomless infinity,
At least a consolation.
. . . There's a gleam of blue that shines
Through a crack in a barn wall—
Here already is your witness: that
Not everything is so plain and flat.

АДАМ

Ленивым взглядом обозрев округу,
Он в самый первый день траву примял,
И лег в тени смоковницы, и, руку
Заведши за голову, задремал.
Он сладко спал. Он спал невозмутимо
Под тишиной эдемской синевы.
...Во сне он видел печи Освенцима
И трупами наполненные рвы.
Своих детей он видел!.. В неге рая
Была улыбка на лице светла.
Дремал он, ничего не понимая,
Не знающий еще добра и зла.

ADAM

Vacantly he stared around him.
That day, his very first, he trampled grass,
Lay down in a fig tree's shade, and placing
His hand behind his head, drowsed off.
And sweetly slept. Slept unperturbed.
Beneath the silence of Eden's blue,
In a dream he saw the ovens of Auschwitz
And the ditches piled with corpses.
It was his children he saw. In Eden's bliss
The smile upon his face was bright.
He slept, and failed to understand,
Unaware as yet of good and evil.

Я

Есть слово «я». И нету в том худого,
Что я решил его произнести.
Оно во мне. Я с детства это слово,
Как после травмы, позабыл почти.

Оно идет из глубины, оттуда,
Чтоб, словно нефть, высоко к небу бить.
Оно — экзема. Нет смертельней зуда
Стремления самим собою быть.

Я слышу дальний голос...

                Смело к краю

Я подхожу, к порогу темноты,
И свешиваюсь вниз, и вопрошаю:
— Кто это там? Он отвечает: ты! —
Но обречен я был бы на молчанье,
Когда вокруг бы не были друзья,
Отец и мать, жена, однополчане,
Попутчики.

             «Мы» состоит из «Я».
Есть слово «Я». Оно во мне недаром
К небытию испытывает злость.
Оно во мне. Оно одним ударом
В меня по шляпку вбито, словно гвоздь.

"I"

There's the word "I." And nothing wrong
In my deciding to pronounce it.
It's in me. As after a trauma, I've almost
Forgotten this word since childhood.

It issues from the depths, from the beyond,
And, like oil, gushes high to heaven.
It's—eczema. There is no ache more
Deadly than the striving to be oneself.

I hear a distant voice . . .
                    Boldly I walk

To the brink, the threshold of darkness,
And lean over, questioning:
"Who's that beyond?" He answers: "Thou!"
But I would have been doomed to silence
If there had been no friends about,
Father and mother, wife, fellow soldiers,
And traveling companions.

            "We" consists of "I."
There's the word "I." No wonder,
In me, it is hostile to non-being.
It's deep within me. At one blow it was hammered
Into me, right up to its head, like a nail.

АВТОБИОГРАФИЯ

А надо мной, как меч дамоклов,
Мой смертный час, и я спешу.
Ведь я свой собственный биограф,—
Я биографию пишу!

Где я родился. Где я вырос,
Чем занимался, где служил...
Рубахи нижней длинный вырез
Мне грудь по пояс обнажил.

Вот мелких дел моих реестр...
Я современник свой живой.
Что делать мне?
               Ведь я свой Нестор,—
Полночный летописец свой.

Кем был. Что значу. И что стою...
Что руку двигает мою?
Черту — помалу — за чертою
Я свой портрет воссоздаю.
Я мог бы обозреть, конечно,
Своих деяний громкий круг.
Как смел я. Как любил я нежно.
Я — как отец. Как муж. Как друг.
Как мудр. И где мои истоки.
Намек на что-то, — остротца́!..
И замер я б навеки в тоге
Неустрашимого борца.

Но откровенности кривая
Несет. Во мне тоска живет,
Грудь перед миром раскрывая,
Как пред анатомом живот.

AUTOBIOGRAPHY

And above me, like the sword of Damocles,
My hour of death, and I am in a hurry.
For I'm my own biographer—
I'm writing my biography.

Where I was born. Where I grew up.
What I did. Where served . . .
The deep cut of my T-shirt
Has exposed my chest to the waist.

Here is the register of my small acts.
I am my own living contemporary.
What shall I do?
           For I'm my own Nestor—
My own midnight chronicler.

Who was I? What do I signify? And what my price . . .
What moves my hand?
Gradually—trait by trait,
I create my own portrait.
I could review, of course,
The noisy circle of my acts.
How I dared. How, tenderly, I loved.
I, as father. As husband. As friend.
How wise I am. And where my sources are.
A mere hint at something—That's real wit! . . .
And I would have stood still forever
In the toga of a fearless fighter.

But the graph of frank revelation
Bears me on. In me nostalgia lives,
Baring my chest for all to see,
As an anatomist cuts a belly open.

ROBERT ROZHDESTVENSKY

1932–

Robert Rozhdestvensky first drew attention to himself as a poet at the age of twenty-three when his poem "My Love" appeared in the magazine *Oktyabr* in 1955. That same year he published his first book of poems, *The Flags of Spring*. Since then Rozhdestvensky has published steadily and has at least eight books to his credit. He is romantic in temperament and writes somewhat in the style of Mayakovsky, though he lacks the latter's power of vision and strength of imagery. He makes a slighter impression than his contemporary Yevtushenko. He is also more conservative in outlook. Nevertheless, he has a distinct lyrical vein of his own and is one of the poets who, in the last decade, has expressed some of the new aspirations of the younger generation.

Robert Rozhdestvensky had a rather troubled childhood. During the war both his parents went to the front, leaving him with his grandmother, who died soon after. He was then brought up in various children's homes. Rozhdestvensky finally succeeded in obtaining a university education in Petrozavodsk and then attended the Gorky Literary Institute in Moscow. He has done a great deal of traveling in Siberia and Soviet Asia and has twice visited the United States. He also happens to be a sportsman and takes part in athletic competitions.

НЕОБИТАЕМЫЕ ОСТРОВА

Снятся усталым спортсменам
                    рекорды,
снятся суровым поэтам
                    слова.
Снятся влюбленным
в огромном городе
необитаемые
            острова.
Самые дальние,
самые тайные,
ветру открытые с трех сторон,
необнаруженные,
необитаемые,
принадлежащие тем,
                кто влюблен.

Даже отличник
            очень старательный
их не запомнит со школьной скамьи, —
ведь у влюбленных
своя
        география!
Ведь у влюбленных
карты
        свои!
Пусть для неверящих
                это в новинку, —
только любовь
предъявила
права.
Верьте:
        не сказка,
верьте:
        не выдумка —
необитаемые острова!..

UNINHABITED ISLANDS

Tired sportsmen dream
                    of records.
Exacting poets dream
                    of words.
In the vast city
lovers dream
of uninhabited
                    islands.
The most distant,
the most secret,
on three sides open to the wind,
undiscovered,
uninhabited,
the property of those
                    who are in love.

Even the bright
                    diligent top pupil
won't remember them in class—
for lovers
have
     their own geography!
For lovers
have
     their own maps!
Let this be a novelty
                    to unbelievers—
but love
has asserted
its rights.
If you believe,
          then this is no fairy tale.
If you believe,
          then this is no fiction—
these uninhabited islands! . . .

Все здесь простое.
Все самое первое —
ровная,
        медленная река,
тонкие-тонкие,
белые-белые,
длинные-длинные
               облака.

Ветры,
которым под небом не тесно.
Птицы,
поющие нараспев.
Море,
бессонное,
          словно сердце.
Горы,
уверенные в себе.
Здесь водопады
         литые,
             летящие,
мягкая,
трепетная трава...

Только для любящих
             по-настоящему
эти
великие острова!..
Двое на острове.
Двое на острове.
Двое — и всё!..
А над ними —
         гроза.

Двое —
        и небо тысячеверстное.

All things are simple here.
All things topnotch—
the smooth
            slow river,
the slender-slender,
white-white
long-long
            clouds.

The winds
that move freely beneath the sky.
The birds
continuing their sing-song.
The sea
as sleepless
            as the heart.
The mountains
certain of themselves.
Here are waterfalls
                of solid cast,
                        flying,
the soft
undulating grass . . .

These
great islands
are only reserved for those
                who are truly in love!
Two on an island.
Two on an island.
Two—and that's all! . . .
and above them
            a storm.

Two—
        and a thousand-mile sky.

Двое — и вечность!
И звезды в глаза...
Это не просто.
Это не просто.
Это сложнее любого
                    в сто крат...

В городе стихшем
на перекрестках
                    желтым огнем
                                    светофоры горят.
Меркнет
        оранжевый облеск
                    неона.

Гаснут рекламы,
гуденье прервав...

Тушатся окна,
тушатся окна
в необитаемых
            островах.

Я уехал
        от весны,
от весенней кутерьмы,
от сосулечной
апрельской
очень мокрой
бахромы.
Я уехал от ручьев,
от мальчишеских боев,
от нахохлившихся почек
и нахальных воробьев,

Two—and eternity!
And stars in the eyes . . .
Not simple this.
Not simple.
A hundredfold
          more complicated . . .

In the hushed city
the traffic lights
        glow yellow
                at the crossroads.
The orange gleam
        of neon
           grows dimmer.

The electric signs go out,
interrupting the hum . . .

The windows turn dark,
the windows turn dark
on the uninhabited
           islands.

1962

I DEPARTED

I departed
        from the spring,
from all the springtime hulabaloo,
from all the icicle-like
April-like
very sodden
fringes.
I departed from the rivulets,
from fisticuffs with the boys,
from the swelling buds
and the cheeky little sparrows,

от стрекота сорочьего,
от нервного брожения,
от головокружения
и прочего,
и прочего...

Отправляясь в дальний путь
на другой конец страны,
думал:

«Ладно!
Как-нибудь
проживем и без весны...
Мне-то в общем
                все равно —
есть она
иль нет ее.
Самочувствие мое
будет неизменным...»

Но...
за семь тысяч верст,
                в Тикси,
прямо среди бела дня
догнала
весна
меня
и сказала:
                «Грязь меси!»
Догнала, растеребя,
                в будни ворвалась
                                и в сны.

from the chattering of the magpies,
from all the nervous restlessness,
from all the giddy headiness,
and this and that,
and this and that . . .

Going off on a distant journey
to the far end of the land,
I thought:

"All right!"
We'll manage
somehow to survive without the spring . . .
On the whole,
              it's all the same—
whether spring
is there or not.
It won't change
the way I feel.

But . . .
even miles away,
              in Tiksi,
right in the middle of the day
the spring
caught up
with me
and said:
       "Wallow through the mud!"
Caught up, plucked me asunder,
                         bursting into my daily life
                              and sleep.

Я уехал
от весны...
Я
уехал
от тебя.
Я уехал в первый раз
от твоих огромных глаз,
от твоих горячих рук,
от звонков твоих подруг,
от твоих горючих слез
самолет меня
унес.
Думал:
«Ладно!
Не впервой!
Покажу
характер свой.
Хоть на время
убегу...
Я ведь сильный,
я
смогу!...»

Я не мерил высоты.
Чуть видна земля была...
Но увидел вдруг:
вошла
в самолет летящий
ты!
В ботах,
            в стареньком пальто...
И сказала:
«Знаешь что?
Можешь не убегать!
Все равно у тебя из этого
    ничего не получится...»

I departed
from the spring.
I
departed
from you.
For the first time I departed
from your enormous eyes,
from your burning hands,
from the telephone calls of your girl companions,
from your scalding tears
the plane
             has taken me away.
I thought:
"All right!
            It's not the first time!
I'll show you
            what my character is like.
I'll run away
            just for a little while . . .
For I am strong,
I
can do it! . . ."

I wasn't thinking of the altitude.
We could hardly see the earth . . .
But suddenly I saw
you entering
the flying
plane!
You wore overboots,
                an old overcoat . . .
And you said to me:
"Do you know?
You needn't run away!
Nothing
        will come of this anyway . . ."

YEVGENY YEVTUSHENKO

1933-

Although Yevgeny Yevtushenko published his first book, *The Prospectors of the Future* in 1952, it was his long poem *Winter Station* (1956) that particularly attracted attention to him as the new poetic voice of the Fifties. In his poem he was concerned with reassessing values, political, social and aesthetic, in the post-Stalinist world. Since then he has been, despite some setbacks, in the very avangard of protesting Soviet youth who want to restore a sense of conscience and greater freedom in literary and public affairs. Yevtushenko has certainly been the boldest among those who insisted on speaking out about the past and present of his country. In his *Babii Yar* (1961), which has not yet been included in any of his volumes, he raised the question of Jewish persecution in Russia. And in his *Letter To Yesenin* (1965), he has even challenged the authority of the Komsomol leader in matters of literature. However, though defending the rights of the poets and helping to clear the ground for the advance of other poets, Yevtushenko is not entirely concerned with criticism and declarative statements. He has a fine and intimate lyrical vein of his own, and this lyrical vein sometimes dominates even in his more social poems such as *Babii Yar* and *The Heirs of Stalin*. He is also a great champion of the ordinary man and has a tender heart for suffering humanity. His *A Precious Autobiography* (1963), the publication of which in Paris got him into so much trouble, reveals many of the aspirations of the new Soviet poets as well as of Soviet youth in general. After a period of silence, he has, since September 1963, published many new cycles of poems.—Yevtushenko was born in Siberia. His childhood was difficult, but he completed his education in Moscow. He graduated from the Gorky Literary Institute. Since 1956 he has been in the vanguard of Soviet poetry. He has traveled extensively and visited the United States. His latest book is *What Is Happening To Me* (1966).

М. Рощину

Я что-то часто замечаю,
к чьему-то, видно, торжеству,
что я рассыпанно мечтаю,
что я растрепанно живу.
Среди совсем нестрашных с виду
полужеланий,
                                получувств
щемит:
                        неужто я не выйду,
неужто я не получусь?
Меня тревожит встреч напрасность,
что и ни сердцу, ни уму,
и та не праздничность,
                                        а праздность,
в моем гостящая дому,
и недоверье к многим книжкам,
и в настроеньях разнобой,
и подозрительное слишком
неупоение собой...

Со всем, чем раньше жил, порву я,
забуду разную беду,
на землю, теплую,
                                парную,
раскинув руки,
                                упаду.
О те, кто наше поколенье!
Мы лишь ступень, а не порог.
Мы лишь вступленье во вступленье,
к прологу новому пролог!
О мой ровесник,
                                друг мой верный!
Моя судьба —
                        в твоей судьбе.

THERE'S SOMETHING I OFTEN NOTICE

TO M. ROSHCHIN

There's something I often notice,
and someone apparently gloats over this,
that I'm rather scatter-brained,
and untidy in my way of living.
Among the, in appearance, harmless
half-desires
   and half-feelings,
my pinching worry is:
      I do all right?
What if I don't pull through?
I am disturbed by all the waste of meetings
that nourish neither heart nor mind,
by the sloth,
   not the festive spirit,
that has taken lodging in my house;
by my mistrust for many books,
and the warring strains in all my moods,
and the far too suspect
non-enthusiasm for myself . . .

I'll break with all I lived with up to now,
forget my various mishaps,
with arms spread out
    fall down
on the warm
   and steamy earth.
Oh those who are my generation!
We're not the threshold, just a step.
We're but the preface to a preface,
a prologue to a newer prologue!
Oh you in years my equal,
     my true friend!
My fate's
  contained in yours.

Давай же будем откровенны
и скажем правду о себе.
Тревоги наши вместе сложим,
себе расскажем и другим,
какими быть уже не можем,
какими быть уже хотим.
Жалеть не будем об утрате,
самодовольство разлюбя.

Завязывается
                характер
с тревоги первой за себя.

КАРЬЕРА

Ю. Васильеву

Твердили пастыри, что вреден
и неразумен Галилей.
Но, как показывает время,
кто неразумней — тот умней.

Ученый — сверстник Галилея
был Галилея не глупее.
Он знал, что вертится Земля,
но у него была семья.

И он, садясь с женой в карету,
свершив предательство свое,
считал, что делает карьеру,
а между тем губил ее.

За осознание планеты
шел Галилей один на риск,

Then let us be extremely frank,
and speak the truth about ourselves.
Let us share our anxieties together,
discuss between us, tell others too,
what sort of men we can't be any longer,
what sort of men we now desire to be.
Fallen out of love with self-conceit,
we shall not regret the loss.

Character
            begins to form
at the first pinch of anxiety about ourselves.

1953

A CAREER

TO YU. VASILIEV

Galileo, the clergy maintained,
was a pernicious and stubborn man.
But time has a way of demonstrating
the most stubborn are the most intelligent.

In Galileo's day, a fellow scientist
was no more stupid than Galileo.
He was well aware the earth revolved,
but he also had a large family to feed.

Stepping into a carriage with his wife,
after effecting his betrayal,
he believed he was launched on a career,
though he was undermining it in reality.

Galileo alone had risked asserting
the truth about our planet,

и стал великим он... Вот это —
я понимаю — карьерист!

Итак, да здравствует карьера,
когда карьера такова,
как у Шекспира и Пастера,
Ньютона и Толстого... Льва!

Зачем их грязью покрывали?
Талант — талант, как ни клейми.
Забыты те, кто проклинали,
но помнят тех, кого кляли.

Все те, кто рвались в стратосферу,
врачи, что гибли от холер,
вот эти делали карьеру!
Я с их карьер беру пример!

Я верю в их святую веру.
Их вера — мужество мое.
Я делаю себе карьеру
тем, что не делаю ее!

and this made him a great man . . . His was
a genuine career as I understand it.

I salute then a career,
when the career is akin to
that of a Shakespeare or Pasteur,
a Newton or Tolstoy—Leo!

Why did people fling mud at them all?
Talent speaks for itself, whatever the charges.
We've forgotten the men who abused them,
Remember only the victims of slander.

All who rushed into the stratosphere,
the doctors who perished fighting cholera,
were, all of them, men of career!
I take their careers as my example!

I believe in their sacred faith.
Their faith is my very manhood.
I shall therefore pursue my career
by trying not to pursue one.

1957

Свежести!
        Свежести!
Хочется свежести!
Свадебной снежности
и незаслеженности,
свежести мускулов,
мозга,
мазка,
свежести музыки
и языка!
Чтоб не держалось,
а провалилось
все, что слежалось
и пропылилось.
Чтоб с неизбежностью
просто
и быстро
свержено
свежестью
все это было.
Много ли проку
в том,
как возятся
те,
кто против
свежего воздуха?
Кем это сдержится?
Это не сдержится!
Свежести!
        Свежести!
Хочется свежести!

FRESHNESS

Freshness!
            Freshness!
We want freshness!
Pure nuptial snow,
and no old tracks,
freshness of muscle,
brain,
          brush stroke,
freshness in music
and language!
May all things long-lain,
crusted with dust,
crumble away,
and not stay there stale.
May freshness
with all inevitability
very simply
              and quickly
displace
          all this.
What's the use
their making
                a fuss—
those
        who object
to fresh air?
Who will maintain it?
It won't be sustained!
Freshness!
            Freshness!
We want freshness!

1960

АМЕРИКАНСКИЙ СОЛОВЕЙ

В стране перлона и дакрона
и ставших фетишем наук
я вдруг услышал кровный-кровный
неповторимо чистый звук.
Для ветки птица — не нагрузка,
и на одной из тех ветвей
сидел и пел он, словно русский, —
американский соловей.
Он пел печально и счастливо,
и кто-то, буйствуя, исторг
ему в ответ сирени взрывы —
земли проснувшийся восторг.
То было в Гарварде весеннем.
В нем все летело кверху дном —
в смеющемся и карусельном,
послеэкзаменно хмельном.
Студенты пели и кутили,
и все, казалось, до основ
смешалось в радужном коктейле
из птиц, студентов и цветов.
Гремел он гордо, непреложно,
тот соловей, такой родной,
над полуправдою и ложью,
над суетливой говорней,
над всеми черными делами,
над миллионами анкет
и над акульими телами
готовых к действию ракет.
А где-то в глубине российской
такой же маленький пострел,
свой клювик празднично раскрывший,
его братишка русский пел.
В Тамбове, Гарварде, Майами
на радость сел и городов

THE AMERICAN NIGHTINGALE

In the land of perlon and dacron,
and of science that has become a fetish,
I suddenly heard a kindred, kindred sound—
a sound quite inimitable and pure.
A branch can easily bear a bird,
and on one of those branches
this American nightingale was perched,
singing just like a Russian nightingale.
Mournfully he sang, and happily,
and someone stormily unleashed
flashes of lilac clusters in reply—
this earth's awakening joy.
This was in Harvard in the spring.
There everything was topsy-turvy—
in laughing Harvard's merry-go-round,
swaying drunkenly after the exams.
The students sang, out on a spree,
and to their foundations all things
seemed mixed in a rainbow cocktail
of students, birds, and flowers.
Proudly, unfailingly, that nightingale—
that so kindred nightingale—thundered
above the half-truths and the lies,
above all the restless chatter,
above all the black deeds,
above the millions of questionnaires
and the shark-like bodies
waiting for rockets to spring into action.
And somewhere in the heart of Russia
the same sort of little scamp,
festively opening his small beak,
his little Russian brother sang.
In Tambov, Harvard, and Miami,
for the delight of villages and cities,

под наливными соловьями
сгибались ветви всех садов.
Хлестала музыка, как вьюга,
с материка на материк...
Все соловьи поймут друг друга.
У них везде один язык.
Поют все тоньше, все нежнее
в единстве трепетном своем...
А мы-то, люди, неужели
друг друга так и не поймем?!

БАБИЙ ЯР

Над Бабьим Яром памятников нет.
Крутой обрыв, как грубое надгробье.
Мне страшно.
                    Мне сегодня столько лет,
как самому еврейскому народу.
Мне кажется сейчас —
                    я иудей.
Вот я бреду по древнему Египту.
А вот я, на кресте распятый, гибну,
и до сих пор на мне — следы гвоздей.
Мне кажется, что Дрейфус —
                              это я.
Мещанство —
              мой доносчик и судья.
Я за решеткой.
                  Я попал в кольцо.
Затравленный,
              оплеванный,
                          оболганный.
И дамочки с брюссельскими оборками,
визжа, зонтами тычут мне в лицо.

the branches in all the gardens bent
beneath the nightingales in ecstasy.
The music, like a blizzard, lashed
one continent and then another . . .
All nightingales will understand each other;
everywhere they speak one language.
In their tremulous union,
they sing ever higher, more tenderly.
But we men, shall we never
understand each other?!

Harvard, U.S.A., 1961 [1962]

BABII YAR

No monument stands over Babii Yar.
A drop sheer as a crude gravestone.
I am afraid.
        Today I am as old in years
as all the Jewish people.
Now I seem to be
        a Jew.
Here I plod through ancient Egypt.
Here I perish crucified, on the cross,
and to this day I bear the scars of nails.
I seem to be
        Dreyfus.
The Philistine
        is both informer and judge.
I am behind bars.
        Beset on every side.
Hounded,
        spat on,
        slandered.
Squealing, dainty ladies in flounced Brussels lace
stick their parasols into my face.

Мне кажется —

я мальчик в Белостоке.
Кровь льется, растекаясь по полам.
Бесчинствуют вожди трактирной стойки
и пахнут водкой с луком пополам.
Я, сапогом отброшенный, бессилен.
Напрасно я погромщиков молю.
Под гогот:
«Бей жидов, спасай Россию!»
Лабазник избивает мать мою.
О, русский мой народ! —

Я знаю —

ты

по сущности интернационален.
Но часто те, чьи руки не чисты,
твоим чистейшим именем бряцали.
Я знаю доброту моей земли.
Как подло,

что, и жилочкой не дрогнув,
антисемиты пышно нарекли
себя «Союзом русского народа»!
Мне кажется —

я — это Анна Франк,
прозрачная,

как веточка в апреле.
И я люблю.

И мне не надо фраз.
Мне надо,

чтоб друг в друга мы смотрели.
Как мало можно видеть,

обонять!
Нельзя нам листьев

и нельзя нам неба.
Но можно очень много —

это нежно
друг друга в темной комнате обнять.

I seem to be then
                    a young boy in Byelostok.
Blood runs, spilling over the floors.
The bar-room rabble-rousers
give off a stench of vodka and onion.
A boot kicks me aside, helpless.
In vain I plead with these pogrom bullies.
While they jeer and shout,
                    "Beat the Yids. Save Russia!"
some grain-marketeer beats up my mother.
O my Russian people!
                    I know
                         you
are international to the core.
But those with unclean hands
have often made a jingle of your purest name.
I know the goodness of my land.
How vile these antisemites—
                    without a qualm
they pompously called themselves
"The Union of the Russian People"!
I seem to be
            Anne Frank
transparent
            as a branch in April.
And I love.
            And have no need of phrases.
My need
        is that we gaze into each other.
How little we can see
                    or smell!
We are denied the leaves,
                    we are denied the sky.
Yet we can do so much—
                    tenderly
embrace each other in a darkened room.

Сюда идут?
          Не бойся — это гулы
самой весны —
          она сюда идет.
Иди ко мне.
          Дай мне скорее губы.
Ломают дверь?
          Нет — это ледоход...
Над Бабьим Яром шелест диких трав.
Деревья смотрят грозно,
          по-судейски.
Все молча здесь кричит,
          и, шапку сняв,
я чувствую,
          как медленно седею.
И сам я,
          как сплошной беззвучный крик,
над тысячами тысяч погребенных.
Я —
          каждый здесь расстрелянный
          старик.
Я —
          каждый здесь расстрелянный
          ребенок.
Ничто во мне
          про это не забудет!
«Интернационал»
          пусть прогремит,
когда навеки похоронен будет
последний на земле антисемит.
Еврейской крови нет в крови моей.
Но ненавистен злобой заскорузлой
я всем антисемитам, как еврей.
И потому —
          я настоящий русский!

They're coming here?
                    Be not afraid. Those are the booming
sounds of spring:
                    spring is coming here.
Come then to me.
                    Quick, give me your lips.
Are they smashing down the door?
                    No, it's the ice cracking . . .
The wild grasses rustle over Babii Yar.
The trees look ominous,
                    like judges.
Here all things scream silently,
                    and, baring my head,
I slowly feel myself
                    turning gray.
And I myself
            am one massive, soundless scream
above the thousand thousand buried here.
I am
      each old man
                    here shot dead.
I am
      every child
                    here shot dead.
Nothing in me
            shall ever forget!
The "Internationale," let it
                    thunder
when the last antisemite on earth
is buried forever.
In my blood there is no Jewish blood.
In their callous rage, all antisemites
must hate me now as a Jew.
For that reason
            I am a true Russian!

September 19, 1961

ЖЕНЩИНА И МОРЕ

Над морем —
                молнии.
Из глубины
взмывают мордами
                    к ним
        лобаны.
Нас в лодке пятеро.
За пядью —
                пядь.
А море спятило,
                относит вспять.
Доцентик химии
под ливнем плещущим
так прячет
            хилые
свои плечики.
Король пинг-понга
в техасских джинсах
вдруг,
        как поповна,
крестясь,
ложится.
Культурник Миша
дрожит,
        как мышь.
Где его мышцы?
Что толку с мышц?!
Все смотрят жертвенно,
держась за сердце...

И вдруг —
            та женщина
на весла села!
И вот над веслами,

THE WOMAN AND THE SEA

Flashes of lightning
                  light the sea.
Out of the depths
the mullets raise
               their gullets of foam
towards them.
There were five of us in the boat.
Hand over hand
              we advance.
But the sea then beat a retreat,
                     sweeping us back.
Under the lashing shower,
the chemistry lecturer
huddles,
        hiding
his skinny shoulders.
The ping pong king
in his Texas jeans
suddenly
          lies down,
fervently blessing himself,
like any parish priest's wife.
Misha the gymnast
trembles
        like a mouse.
Where are his biceps?
What good his muscles here?
All three gape like scapegoats,
each clutching at his heart . . .

But all of a sudden
                that woman
sat down to the oars!
And above the oars then,

над кашей чертовой
возникли волосы,
как факел черный!
Вошла ей в душу
игра —
игла.
Рыбачкой дюжей
она гребла.
Гребла загадка
для волн
            и нас,
вся —
        из загара
и рыжих глаз!
Ей,
    медной,
            мокрой,
простой,
'как Маугли,
                и мало —
молний!
и моря —
мало!

Всего, что било,
всего, что мяло,
ей мало было!
да!
    мало!
        мало!

Уже не барышней,
сопя подчеркнуто,
доцентик
        баночкой
полез вычерпывать.
Король пинг-понга
под рев неистовый
вдруг стал
            приподнято

above the devil's own brew,
a mass of hair loomed
like a black torch!
And the sport of it,
needle-like, bit
deep into her soul.
Like a sturdy fisherman,
she rowed on.
Rowed on, an enigma
to the waves
     and to us,
in appearance
      all tan
and reddish eyes!
For her,
    bronzed,
    drenched,
simple
   as Mowgli,
the lightning's
     not too big!
The sea's
   not too big!

All that was battering us,
All that was crumpling us,
wa's not too big for her!
No!
   not too big!
      not too big!

Girlish no longer,
sniffling emphatically,
the lecturer
    now crawled
to bail out with a can.
To the horrendous howling,
the ping-pong king
of a sudden began,
     raising his voice,

свой «рок» насвистывать.
Культурник вспомнил,
что он —
      мужчина...

Всех,
    с морем в споре,
она
   учила!
А море бухало
о буты
    бухты.
Мы были
     будто
бунт
    против бунта!

Летя сквозь волны,
расставшись с жестами,
мы были —
     воины,
и вождь наш —
      женщина!

В любые трудности,
в любые сложности,
когда по трусости
мы станем ежиться, —
на все пошедшие,
сильны,
    смешливы,
напомнят женщины,
что мы —
     мужчины!
Всего, что мяло
и что ломало,
нам станет мало!
Да —
   мало!
     мало!

to whistle his "rock and roll."
The gymnast remembered
he was

    a man.

She lessoned

       us all,
who scuffled

       with the sea!
And the seas kept battering
against the rocks

       of the bay.
And we seemed

       to be
in revolt

       against a rebellion!

Flying through the waves,
our gestures left behind,
we now

       were warriors,
and a woman

       was our chief!

In moments of stress,
complication and distress,
when out of cowardice,
we begin to squirm,
then women who dared all,
who are strong,
and like to laugh,
will remind us
that we

       are men!
All that was crumpling us,
all that was battering us,
will prove not too big!
No!

    not too big!

        not too big!

1962

ПЕСНЯ НАДСМОТРЩИКОВ

Мы — надсмотрщики,
мы —
      твои ножки,
           трон.
При виде нас
         морщится
брезгливо
      фараон.
А что он без нас?
Без наших глаз?
Без наших глоток?
Без наших плеток?
Плетка —
      лекарство,
хотя она не мед.
Основа государства —
надсмотр,
надсмотр.
Народ без назидания
работать бы не смог.
Основа созиданья —
надсмотр,
      надсмотр.
И воины, раскиснув,
бежали бы, как сброд.
Основа героизма —
надсмотр,
      надсмотр.
Опасны, кто задумчивы.
Всех мыслящих —
          к закланью.
Надсмотр за душами
важней,
      чем за телами.
Вы что-то загалдели?
Вы снова за нытье?

THE SONG OF THE OVERSEERS

We are the overseers.
We are
    your legs,
        O throne.
At the sight of us
        the Pharaoh
squeamishly
        turns up his nose.
But what is he without us?
Without our eyes?
Without our throats?
Without our whips?
The lash
    is good medicine,
though not as sweet as honey.
The foundation of the state—
is overseeing,
        overseeing.
Without exhortation, the people
could not work.
The basis of creation
is overseeing,
        overseeing.
And warriors, turned sour,
would scatter like a rabble.
The foundation of heroism
is overseeing,
        overseeing.
Thoughtful men are dangerous.
Those who think
        must be immolated.
It is more important to oversee
souls
    than bodies.
You're shouting again?
You're complaining again?

Свободы захотели?
А разве нет ее?!
(И звучат не слишком бодро
голоса:
              «Есть!

                     Есть!» —
то ли есть у них свобода,
то ли хочется им есть.)
Мы —
        надсмотрщики.
Мы гуманно грубые.
Мы вас бьем не до смерти,
для вашей пользы, глупые.
Плетками
            по черным

                          спинам
рубя,
внушаем:
            «Почетна
работа
          раба».
Что о свободе грезить?
Имеете вы, дурни,
свободу —
            сколько влезет
молчать,
            о чем вы думаете.
Мы — надсмотрщики.
С нас тоже
            пот ручьем.
Рабы,
        вы нас не можете
упрекнуть
            ни в чем.
Мы смотрим настороженно.
Мы псы —
            лишь без намордников.

Is it freedom you want?
But don't you already have it?!
(And not-too-confident voices
reply:
   "We have it!
      We have it!"
but have they freedom
or do they want to eat?)
We are
   the overseers.
We are humanely brutal.
We don't thrash you to death,
we lash you for your own good, you dolts.
Welting
   black
     backs
with our whips,
we suggest:
   "The work
a slave does
   is honorable."
Why dream of freedom?
Fools, you have
the freedom—
   as much as you can take,
to keep your mouths shut
     about what you're thinking.
We are the overseers.
We also sweat
   in streams.
Slaves,
  there's no reproach
you can make
   against us.
Our eyes are watchful.
We're hounds—
   but have no muzzles.

Но ведь и мы,
          надсмотрщики, —
рабы других надсмотрщиков.
И над рабами стонущими,
раб Амона он —
надсмотрщик всех надсмотрщиков,
наш бедный фараон...

ИСКУССТВО

Мне сказал монтажник Слава Лучкин:
«Ну-ка, парень, сядь и закури!
Знаю, есть писатели и лучше,
но люблю я Сент-Экзюпери.

И порою кажется мне ночью:
в самолете пристальном своем
все летает этот чертов летчик
и следит за тем, как мы живем».

Мы молчали в сумраке таежном.
Было еще долго до зари,
и мерцала ГЭС крылом тревожным
самолета Сент-Экзюпери...

Мне сказал прораб Спартак Сорокин:
«Я на водку время не гублю.
Век у нас, по-моему, серьезный —
музыку серьезную люблю.

И, скидая грязную рубаху,
лишь с работы вечером вернусь,
я бросаюсь к Шуберту и Баху,
к Скрябину и Мусоргскому рвусь.

But we,
>> the overseers,
are slaves to other overseers.
And above the groaning slaves
stands Amon's slave—
the overseer of all overseers,
our poor Pharaoh . . .

1965

ART

Slava Luchkin, the fitter, said to me:
"Well, young fellow, sit down and smoke!
I know there are some better writers,
But I personally love Saint-Exupéry.

"At times in the night, it seems to me,
this daredevil aviator is still piloting
his steadfast plane, closely observing
the way we go about our life."

In the taiga's dusk we sat in silence.
It was still a long while to dawn.
And the GES glimmered like a quivering
wing of Saint-Exupéry's plane.

Spartak Sorokin, the foreman, declared:
"I don't waste any time on vodka.
As I see it, we live in a serious age—
and I am fond of serious music.

"As soon as I get home from work,
I pull off my dirty shirt,
and rush to Bach and Schubert,
grab at Scriabin and Moussorgsky.

И лежу, и кружатся пластинки,
ну, а у дверей, оцепенев,
как щенята, слушают ботинки,
на которых глина и цемент...»

И сказала мне конструктор Клава
около старинного скита:
«У меня есть что-то вроде клада —
тоненькие книжечки «Скира».

Вижу я в тайге сады Гогена
и Сезанна сизые стога.
Брезжут мне сквозь брызги автогена
голубые девочки Дега.

Вы уж за фантазию простите,
но когда метелица свистит,
весь в снегу, роденовский Мыслитель
у плотины на краю сидит...»

И само не знаешь ты, искусство,
что на этом дальнем берегу
светом ты тащило нас из гнуса
к будущему свету сквозь тайгу.

Скалы и деревья мы валили,
да и сами падали без сил,
но свою Кабирию Феллини
к нам на самосвале привозил.

Разделяя с нами все мытарства,
шел Толстой в неистовых снегах,
Достоевский мучился, метался,
Горький брел с ребенком на руках.

И недаром, полная пророчеств,
будто бы бушующая мысль,
ГЭС, ты по-бетховенски рокочешь,
ГЭС, по-маяковски ты гремишь!

"The records spin as I lie down,
and by the doorway a pair of boots,
caked with cement and clay, listen,
like puppies, in rapt attention . . ."

And as we stood by an old monastery,
Klava, a draughtsman, told me:
"I have something like a treasure trove—
the slender volumes Skira published.

"In the taiga I see traces of Gauguin,
and the blue-gray hayricks of Cézanne.
Through the sparks of an acetylene torch
I see the blue ballerinas of Degas.

"You will forgive me my fantasy,
but when the blizzard's shrilling,
Rodin's Thinker, clad in snow,
sits brooding on the brink of the dam . . ."

You yourself, Art, had no notion
that, on this far shore, your glow
has helped to pull us out of the mire,
through the taiga, to the light of the future.

We blew up rocks and felled tall trees,
and collapsed from sheer exhaustion,
but Fellini brought us his *Cabiria*
in the back of a dumping-truck.

Sharing in all our trials, Tolstoy
walked with us through blinding snowstorms;
Dostoyevsky agonized and tossed;
and Gorky trudged, a new-born in his arms.

Not in vain then, brimming with prophesies
as though you were a storm-charged thought,
GES, you resound like Beethoven,
GES, you thunder forth like Mayakovsky.

1965

МАЯКОВСКИЙ

...И, вставши у подножья Братской ГЭС,
подумал я о Маяковском сразу,
как будто он костисто,
                              крупноглазо
в ее могучем облике воскрес.

Громадный,
              угловатый,
                          как плотина,
стоит он поперек любых неправд,
натруженно,
              клокочуще,
                          партийно,
попискиванья
              грохотом поправ.
Я представляю,
              как бы он дубасил
всех прохиндеев тяжестью строки
и как бы здесь,
              тайгу шатая басом,
читал бы он строителям стихи.
К нему не подступиться с меркой собственной,
                          но, ощущая боль и немоту,
могу представить все,
              но Маяковского
в тридцать седьмом
                          представить не могу.
Что было б с ним,
              когда б тот револьвер
не выстрелил?
              Когда б он жив остался?

MAYAKOVSKY

. . . And standing at the foot of the GES at Bratsk,
I immediately thought of Mayakovsky,
as if, all of bone
               and big-of-eye,
he had been resurrected in its mighty aspect.

Huge,
      angular
            as a dam,
he stands astride all untruths,
straining,
         boiling over,
                party-like,
crushing their squeals
             with his thunder.
I can picture how,
            with his ponderous line,
he would have drubbed all the scoundrels;
and how, on this spot,
              shaking the taiga with his deep voice,
he would have read his poems to the construction workers.
He can't be measured in a personal way,
                but, feeling pained and numb,
I can imagine all sorts of things,
              but what's hard to imagine
is Mayakovsky
         in the year 1937.
What would have happened to him,
               if that revolver
had not gone off?
        If he had remained alive?

Быть может, поразумнел?

                Поправел?

Тому, что ненавидел, все же сдался?

А может,

        он ушел бы мрачно в сторону,

молчал,

      зубами скрежеща,

                вдали,

                      когда ночами где-то

в «черных воронах»

большевиков расстреливать везли?

Не верю!

      Несгибаемо,

              таранящe

он встал бы и обрушил

            вещий гром,

и, в мертвых ставший

           «лучшим

             и талантливейшим»,

в живых —

          он был объявлен бы врагом.

А если бы тот выстрел не

                раздался, —

себе наград и славы не ища,

как многие,

        он честен бы остался,

эпоху на плечах своих таща.

Нет,

      он бы не поддался,

            не сломился —

он, как проходчик,

          вел бы нас вперед.

К сражениям,

        а не к самоубийству

всей жизнью

          Маяковский нас зовет.

Пусть до конца тот выстрел не разгадан,

в себя ли он стрелять нам дал пример?

Perhaps, he'd be reasonable?
                    More conservative?
Yielded to what he hated so much?
But, perhaps,
            he'd have sullenly turned aside,
kept his counsel,
            grinding his teeth
                    at a distance,
                            when in the night
Black Marias
drove bolsheviks away to be shot?
But this I believe!
            Unbending,
                ram-like,
he'd have risen up and pealed
                in prophetic thunder.
And having become, in death,
                "the best
                and most talented,"
he would have been declared "an enemy"
                    had he lived.
And if that shot
            had not rung out,
seeking no award, no fame,
like so many others,
            he'd have remained honest,
and carried the age on his shoulders.
No,
    he'd not have yielded,
                not been broken—
even as a drifter
            he'd have led us forward.
By his whole life,
            Mayakovsky summons us
to fight,
        not to commit suicide.
Even if that shot has not been fully explained,
did he set us an example of shooting ourselves?

Стреляет снова,

рокоча раскатом,

над веком вознесенный револьвер —

тот револьвер,

испытанный на прочность,

из прошлого,

как будто с двух шагов,

стреляет в тупость,

в лицемерье,

в пошлость:

в невыдуманных —

подлинных врагов.

Он учит против лжи,

все так же косной,

за дело революции стоять.

В нем нам оставил пули Маяковский,

чтобы стрелять,

стрелять,

стрелять,

стрелять.

«ДА» И «НЕТ»

(Из стихов о любви)

Я, как поезд,

что мечется столько уж лет

между городом «Да»

и городом «Нет».

Мои нервы натянуты,

как провода,

между городом «Нет»

и городом «Да».

Нет любви в этом городе «Нет».

Он похож

на обитый тоской кабинет.

По утрам

натирают в нем желчью паркет.

В нем насупился замкнуто

каждый предмет.

It shoots again,
>   out of the past,
>   that revolver,
tested for precision,
>   shaking us with its detonation,
as though at two paces;
shoots at crassness,
>   hypocrisy,
>   and vileness:
at real,
>   not imaginary enemies.
It teaches us to oppose falsehood,
>   still so stagnantly there,
to stand up for the cause of the Revolution.
Mayakovsky left us some bullets
>   in that revolver,
bullets for us to shoot,
>   shoot,
>   shoot,
>   shoot.

1965

"YES" AND "NO"

(FROM VERSES ABOUT LOVE)

I'm like a train
>   that's been shuttling for years
between the city of "Yes"
>   and the city of "No."
My nerves strain,
>   like the telegraph wires,
between the city of "No"
>   and the city of "Yes."
There's no love in this city of "No."
It resembles
>   a room upholstered with anguish.
There, in the morning,
>   they polish the parquet with bile.
Each object there
>   sullenly scowls.

В нем диваны —
                из фальши,
в нем стены —
                из бед.
Черта с два
        в нем получишь ты
                        добрый совет,
или, скажем, букет,
                или просто привет.
Пишмашинки стучат
                под копирку ответ:
«Нет-нет-нет...
                нет-нет-нет...
                        нет-нет-нет...»
А когда
        совершенно погасится свет,
начинают в нем призраки
                мрачный балет.
Черта с два —
        хоть подохни! —
                достанешь билет,
чтоб уехать
        из черного города «Нет»...
Ну, а в городе «Да»
                жизнь, как песня дрозда.
Этот город без стен,
                он подобье гнезда.
В руки просится с неба
                любая звезда,
просят губы любые
                твоих
                        без стыда,
бормоча еле слышно:
                «А.... все ерунда!», —
и сорвать себя просит,
                дразня,
                        резеда,

The sofas
            are of spurious material.
The walls—
                of misfortune.
What chance
                of your receiving good counsel,
or, let's say, a bouquet
                    or even a welcome.
All the answer you get
                    is a carbon copy:
"No-no-no . . .
                No-no-no . . .
                        No-no-no . . ."
And when
            the light's completely switched off,
ghosts in that room
                    dance a somber ballet.
What chance—
                try as you may—
                        of getting a ticket
to travel away
                from the black city of "No" . . . ,
But in the city of "Yes,"
                    life's like the song of a thrush.
No walls in this city—
                    it looks like a nest.
Any star of the sky
                just begs to fall in your hands;
lips, any lips,
                unashamed, just ask for your lips,
barely mumbling:
                "Ah, what nonsense this!"
and teasingly the mignonette
                        begs you
                            to pluck it,

и, мыча,

молоко предлагают

стада,

и ни в ком подозрения

нет ни следа,

и, куда ты захочешь,

мгновенно туда

унесут поезда,

самолеты,

суда,

и, журча,

как года,

чуть лепечет вода:

«Да-да-да...

да-да-да...

да-да-да...»

Только скучно,

по правде сказать,

иногда,

что дается мне столько

почти без труда

в разноцветно светящемся

городе «Да»...

Пусть уж лучше мечусь

до конца моих лет

между городом «Да»

и городом «Нет»!

Пусть уж нервы натянуты,

как провода,

между городом «Нет»

и городом «Да»!

and, lowing,
              the herds
                         offer their milk,
and no trace of suspicion
                          lurks in man,
and wherever you might want to go,
                                  instantly
the trains,
          the planes,
                      the ships will take you there.
And babbling
            like the years,
                           the water just lisps:
"Yes-yes-yes . . .
                  Yes-yes-yes . . .
                                   Yes-yes-yes . . ."
It's tedious though,
                    truth to tell,
                                  what I manage to do
at times
        without straining at all
in the multicolored,
                    brightly-lit
                                city of "Yes" . . .
I'd do better to shuttle
                        to the end of my years
between the city of "Yes"
                          and the city of "No"!
Let my nerves strain,
                     like the telegraph wires,
between the city of "No"
                        and the city of "Yes."

1965

ПИСЬМО ЕСЕНИНУ

Поэты русские! Друг друга мы браним,
Парнас российский дрязгами заселен.
Но все мы чем-то связаны родным,
Любой из нас есть чуточку Есенин.

И я Есенин, но совсем иной,
В колхозе от рожденья конь мой розовый.
Я, как Россия, более стальной
И, как Россия, менее березовый.

Есенин, милый, изменилась Русь,
Но плакаться, по-моему, напрасно
И говорить, что к лучшему, боюсь,
И говорить, что к худшему, опасно

Какие стройки, спутники, в стране,
Но потеряли мы в пути неровном
И двадцать миллионов на войне
И миллионы на войне с народом.

Забыть об этом — память отрубить!
Но где топор, что память враз отрубит?
Никто, как русский, не спасал других,
Никто, как русский, сам себя не губит.

Но наш корабль плывет, хоть и мелка вода,
Мы по суху вперед Россию тащим...
Что сволочей хватает — не беда:
Нет Ленина — вот это очень тяжко.

И тяжко то, что нет тебя
И твоего соперника — горлана.
Я вам, конечно, не судья,
Но все-таки ушли вы слишком рано.

LETTER TO YESENIN

Russian Poets! We abuse each other.
The Russian Parnassus is rife with squabbles.
Yet something native binds us all together.
Any one of us is, in part, Yesenin.

And I'm Yesenin too, but wholly different.
My kholhoz horse was rose of hue from birth.
Like Russia, I am now of harder steel
And, like Russia, have less birch in me.

My dear Yesenin, Russia's greatly changed,
But there's no point in weeping over this;
I fear to say the change is for the better;
To say it's "for the worse" is dangerous.

Great work's afoot, we've sputniks in our land!
But on our uneven journey we have lost
Some twenty million people in the war
And millions in the war against the people.

To forget this is to cut off memory!
But where's the axe would chop off memory?
None have saved others as Russians have;
None destroy themselves as Russians do.

But our ship still floats in shallow water,
And we drag Russia forward over land . . .
The many scoundrels are no great matter:
What's hard to bear is Lenin's absence . . .

Your absence, too, is hard to bear, Yesenin,
And that of your great rival—the big bawler.
I haven't come to judge you, it goes without saying,
But all the same you left us far too soon.

Когда румяный комсомольский вождь
На нас, поэтов, кулаком грохочет
И хочет наши думы мять, как воск,
И вылепить свое подобье хочет,

Его слова, Есенин, не страшны,
Но трудно быть от этого веселым...
И мне не хочется, поверь, задрав штаны,
Бежать за этим комсомолом.

Мой комсомол, с кем я в строю хожу,
Кто в Братске строит, на Алтае сеет,
Мой комсомол, за кем бежать хочу, —
Вы: Пушкин, Маяковский и Есенин.

Порою больно мне, и горько это все
И силы нет сопротивляться вздору
И втягивает жизнь под колесо,
Как шарф втянул когда-то Айседору.

Но надо жить... ни водка, ни петля,
Ни женщины — все это не спасенье,
Спасенье ты — российская земля,
Спасенье — искренность твоя, Есенин.

Кто говорит, что ты не из борцов,
Борьба в любой, пусть тихой, но правдивости,
Ты был партийней стольких подлецов,
Пытавшихся учить тебя партийности.

И пронеся гражданственную честь
Сквозь дрязги коммунального Парнаса
Хотя б за то, что в ней Есенин есть,
Я говорю: — Россия — ты прекрасна!

When the pink-cheeked leader of the Komsomol
Thumps with his fist against us poets,
And tries to knead our thoughts like wax,
And wants to mold us in his image,

His words, Yesenin, strike no terror in us,
But this is hardly a cause for being cheerful . . .
Believe me, I've no wish to run
With trousers hitched behind this Komsomol.

The Komsomol, with whom I keep in step,
Are building at Bratsk and sowing in the Altai.
The Komsomol, whom I would follow after,
Are you—Pushkin, Mayakovsky and Yesenin.

I'm hurt at times, and this brings bitter feelings,
And my strength fails when fighting all this nonsense;
Life drags us under the wheel
As a scarf dragged Isadora to her death.

We must live . . . There's no salvation we can find
In vodka, women, or the noose.
It's you will be our saviour, Russian land.
It's your sincerity, Yesenin, that will save us.

Who says you never were a fighting man?
Truth must be fought for, however quiet.
You were more often right than all those scoundrels
Who tried to instil in you the party spirit.

And having borne myself with civic honor
In all the squabbles of our joint Parnassus,
And done so because Yesenin was a poet there,
I state: "Indeed, you're beautiful, my Russia!"

И русская поэзия идет
Вперед сквозь подозренья и нападки
И хваткою Есенинской кладет
Европу, как Поддубный, на лопатки.

ПАМЯТИ ПОЭТА КСЕНИИ НЕКРАСОВОЙ

Я никогда не забуду про Ксюшу,
Ксюшу,
             похожую на простушку,
с глазами косившими,
                         рябоватую,
в чем виноватую?
                   Виноватую
в том, что была рябовата,
                     косила
и некрасивые платья носила...

Что ей от нас было, собственно, надо?
Доброй улыбки
                   стакан лимонада,
да чтоб стихи хоть немножко печатали,
и чтобы приняли Ксюшу в писатели...

Мы лимонада ей, в общем, давали,
ну а вот доброй улыбки —
                              едва ли,
даже давали ей малые прибыли,
только в писатели Ксюшу не приняли,
ибо блюстители наши моральные
определили —
                   она ненормальная...

And Russian poetry goes on advancing
In spite of all suspicion and attack,
And with the sort of hold Yesenin used
It pins, like Poddúbny, Europe on her back.

November 1965

IN MEMORY OF THE POET XENIA NEKRASOVA

I'll never forget about Ksiusha,
Ksiusha,
           who looked so like a ninny,
with her squinting eyes,
                         her pockmarks.
And how was she to blame?
                         Her blame
lay in her pockmarks,
                     her squinting eyes,
and the unsightly dresses she wore . . .

What did she really want of us?
A kindly smile,
               a glass of lemonade,
that we print her verse from time to time
and accept her, Ksiusha, as a writer . . .

In general, we gave her the lemonade,
but as for the kindly smile—
                             hardly that.
We even paid her an occasional small fee,
but we wouldn't accept her as a writer,
because our moral guardians
had decided
           she wasn't normal.

Люди,
          нормальные до отвращения,
вы —
          ненормальные от рождения.
Вам ли понять,
              что, исполнена мужества,
Ксюша была беременна музыкой?

Так и в гробу наша Ксюша лежала.
На животе она руки держала,
будто она охраняла негромко
в нем находящегося ребенка...

Ну а вот вы-то,
              чем вы беременны?
Музыкой, что ли,
              или бореньями?
Что вы кичитесь вашей бесплотностью,
люди,
          беременные бесплодностью?
Вам не простится
              за бедную Ксюшу.
Вам отомстится
              за Ксюшину душу.

You,
>   who are so revoltingly normal,
you
>   are abnormal from birth.
How could you understand that Ksiusha
>   was full of courage
and pregnant with music?

Thus, our Ksiusha lay in her coffin.
She held her hands clasped on her belly,
as though she were gently protecting
an infant in it . . .

But as for you,
>   with what are you pregnant?
With music maybe?
>   Or merely with bones of contention?
Why do you brag of denying your bodies,
you
>   who are pregnant only with barrenness?
You shall not be forgiven
>   on poor Ksiusha's account.
You'll have to pay
>   for Ksiusha's soul.

1965

КОЛИЗЕЙ

Колизей,
            я к тебе не пришел, как в музей.
Я не праздный какой-нибудь ротозей.
Наша встреча —
                  как встреча двух старых друзей
и двух старых врагов,
                  Колизей.
Ты напрасно на гибель мою уповал.
Я вернулся,
         тобою забыт,
как на место,
             где тысячи раз убивал
и где тысячи раз был убит.
Твои львы
          меня гладили лапами —
эта ласка была страшна.
Гладиатору —
            гладиаторово,
Колизей,
        во все времена.
Ты хотел утомленно,
                спесиво,
чтобы я ни за что ни про что
погибал на арене красиво,
но красиво не гибнет никто.
И когда,
        уже копий не чувствуя,
падал я,
        умирая, как зверь,
палец,
      вниз опущенный,
                 чудился
даже в пальце,
         поднятом вверх...

COLISEUM

Coliseum,
            I haven't come to you as to a museum,
I'm no idle gawker.
Our encounter
                is the meeting of two old friends
and two old enemies,
                            Coliseum.
You hoped for my death in vain.
I have returned,
                whom you've forgotten,
as to a place
            where I've killed thousands of times,
and thousands of times have myself been killed.
Your lions
            have stroked me with their paws—
their caresses were terrible.
To a gladiator
                all is gladiatorial,
Coliseum,
            at all times.
Wearily,
            in your conceit you wished
me to perish handsomely in the arena
for no good reason or cause,
but no one perishes handsomely.
And when,
                no longer feeling the spears,
I fell,
        dying like a beast,
a turned down
                thumb
                            seemed
to replace
            even a turned up thumb . . .

Я вернулся, как месть —

                        нету мести грозней.
Ты не ждал, Колизей?

                        Трепещи, Колизей!
И пришел я не днем,

                        а в глубокой ночи,
когда дрыхнут все гиды твои —

                        ловкачи,
а вокруг —

                только запах собачьей мочи,
и жестянки,

                и битые кирпичи...
Но хоть криком кричи,

                        но хоть рыком рычи —
в моем теле

                ворочаются

                        мечи,
и обломки коггей,

                        и обломки страстей...
Снова слышу

                под хруст христианских костей
хруст сластей на трибунах

                        в зубах у детей.
Колизей,

        ты отвык от подобных затей?
Что покажешь сегодня ты мне, Колизей?

Рыщут крысы непуганые
среди царства ночного руинного.
Педерасты напудренные
жмут друг дружку у выхода львиного.
В бывшей ложе Нероновой
дама светская сладостно вздрагивает.
Слышен шелест нейлоновый —
жиголо с нее трусики стягивает.
Там, где пахнет убийствами,

I've returned an avenger—
                        no revenge more dread.
You didn't expect it, Coliseum?
                        Tremble, Coliseum!
And I came not by day,
                        but in the deep of night,
when all your guides had beat it—
                        the dodgers,
and when all around
                        was only the stench of dogs' piss,
abandoned cans
            and broken bricks . . .
But shout your shouts,
                    roar your roars—
in my body
            swords
                    turn and twist,
and fragments of claws
                    and fragments of passions . . .
Again I hear
            the crunch of Christian bones,
the crunch of children's teeth
                    biting candy in the stand.
Coliseum,
            are you disused to such pastimes?
What will you show me today, Coliseum?

Unafraid, rats scour
the ruined nocturnal kingdom.
Pederasts with powdered faces
squeeze each other at the gate to the lion's den.
In Nero's former box
a society lady quivers with lust.
One can hear the rustling of nylon—
a gigolo is pulling off her panties.
Where it smells of murders,

где в земле мои белые косточки,
проститутка по-быстрому
деловито присела на корточки.
Там, где мы, гладиаторы,
гибли, жалкие, горемычные,
кто-то в лица заглядывает:
«Героинчик... Кому героинчика?»

Принимай,
      Колизей,
              безропотно
эту месть
         и судьбу не кори.
Постигает всегда бескровие
все, что зиждется на крови.
Но скажу,
      Колизей,
            без иронии:
я от страха порой холодею.
Только внешнее безнероние
в мире этом —
             сплошном Колизее.
Расщепляют, конечно, атомы,
забираются в звездный простор,
но на зрителей
         и гладиаторов
разделяется мир до сих пор.
Гладиаторов не обижу:
их жалею всей шкурой, нутром, —
ну, а зрителей ненавижу:
в каждом зрителе
           жив Нерон.
Да, страшны

where my white bones lie in the earth,
there a prostitute has squatted down
swiftly, intent on her business.
Where we, the gladiators,
used to perish, poor hapless fellows,
there some one searches our faces:
"Heroin . . . Who wants a little heroin?"

Accept,
      Coliseum,
                without complaint,
this revenge
          and blame not your fate.
Anemia always comes upon
all things founded on blood.
But, Coliseum,
        let me say
             without irony:
At times I freeze with fear.
This world—
        this out-and-out Coliseum,
only seems to have no heroes.
Of course, men smash atoms,
explore starry spaces,
but the world
        to this day
is still split into spectators and gladiators.
I'll not disparage the gladiators:
I pity them with all my hide and innards—
but, well, I hate the spectators:
in each spectator
        a Nero lives.
Yes, they're terrible,

эти зрители сытые,
с мест кричащие:
«Бей!
Коли!»
Ну, а самые страшные зрители —
наживающиеся на крови.
Подстрекатели,
горлодратели,
вы натравливаете без стыда.
Вы хотели б,
чтобы мы,
гладиаторы,
убивали друг друга всегда?!
Улюлюкатели,
науськиватели,
со своих безопасных мест
вы визжите,
чтоб мы не трусили,
чтобы
лезли красиво на меч...
Проклинаю
Нероновы жесты,
только слышите,
подлецы:
в мире есть
палачи и жертвы,
но и есть еще третьи —
борцы!
Я бреду,
голодая по братству,
спотыкаясь, бреду сквозь века,
и во снах моих гладиаторских
вижу нового Спартака.
Вот стою на арене эстрады

these satiated spectators,
who shout from their seats:
"Slash him!
Stab him!"
Well, the most terrible spectators
are those who profit by blood.
Instigators,
loud mouths,
without shame you incite others.
You would like us,
gladiators,
to be always
killing each other?
Hallooers,
hounders,
from your safe seats
you squeal
at us to be fearless,
to spit ourselves
beautifully on a sword . . .
I curse
the Nero-like gestures,
and hear me,
you scoundrels:
in our world there are
victims and executioners,
but there's also a third force—
the fighters!
I wander about,
hungering for brotherhood;
stumbling, I wander through the ages,
and in my gladiatorial dreams
I see a new Spartacus.
There I stand in the arena

перед залом, кипящим, как ад.
Я измотан,
      истрепан,
            изранен,
но не падаю:
        не пощадят.
Львиный рык ожидающий —
                 в рокоте.
Весь театр под когтями трещит.
В меня мечут вопросы,
            как дротики,
ну, а кожа —
        единственный щит.
Колизей,
      аплодируй,
          глазей!
Будь ты проклят,
         палач Колизей!
И спасибо тебе за науку!
Поднимаю
       сквозь крики и визг
над тобою мстящую руку
и безжалостно —
        палец вниз...

before an audience seething as hell.
I'm done for,
                    worn out,
                                    covered with wounds,
but I do not fall:
                    they will not spare me.
Amid the general roar I expect
                                    the lion's growl.
The whole arena crackles beneath the claws.
Questions are hurled at me
                            like javelins,
but, well, my skin's
                    my only shield.
Coliseum,
            applaud,
                        gaze your fill!
May you be accursed,
                        Coliseum-the-executioner!
And thanks for teaching me!
Above the screams and squeals
                                I raise
my avenging hand
and, showing no mercy,
                        turn my thumb down . . .

December 1965

BELLA AKHMADULINA

1937–

Bella Akhmadulina is certainly in the front rank of the younger Soviet poets and is no doubt the outstanding young woman poet. She is the former wife of Yevgeny Yevtushenko, and is now married to Yury Nagibin, the well-known story writer. As her long poem, "My Genealogy" (1964), tells us, she is of mixed Tartar and Italian origin. She was born in one of the worst years of the Stalin purges. She attended and was expelled from the Gorky Literary Institute in 1957 and had some difficulty in getting her poems published in the beginning. Her first and only book to date, *Struna* (*Chord*), appeared in 1962. Since then she has been published more widely in various magazines, especially *Yunost*. Akhmadulina has often been criticized for writing lyrics that are too intimate in tone. However, this preoccupation with individual emotions is part of the new outlook of the sixties. Akhmadulina does inject occasional, though often veiled comments on more public matters. Her earlier lyrics are usually short and classical in form. Of late she has published longer poems such as "My Genealogy" and "Rain." In "Rain" she presents us with a confrontation between the imaginative and irrational elements symbolized by a poet and the "orderly world" of the official great. Rain here is the unexpected, disruptive and yet thirst-quenching element, which seems to shock everybody but the poet.

ПЯТНАДЦАТЬ МАЛЬЧИКОВ

Пятнадцать мальчиков, а, может быть, и больше,
а, может быть, и меньше, чем пятнадцать,
испуганными голосами
мне говорили:
«Пойдем в кино или в музей изобразительных искусств».
Я отвечала им примерно вот что:
«Мне некогда».
Пятнадцать мальчиков дарили мне подснежники.
Пятнадцать мальчиков надломленными голосами
мне говорили:
«Я никогда тебя не разлюблю».
Я отвечала им примерно вот что:
«Посмотрим».

Пятнадцать мальчиков теперь живут спокойно.
Они исполнили тяжелую повинность
подснежников, отчаянья и писем.
Их любят девушки —
иные красивее, чем я,

FIFTEEN BOYS

Fifteen boys and, maybe, more,
or fewer than fifteen, maybe,
said to me
in frightened voices:
"Let's go to a movie or the Museum of Fine Arts."
I answered them more or less like this:
"I haven't time."
Fifteen boys presented me with snowdrops.
Fifteen boys in broken voices
said to me:
"I'll never stop loving you."
I answered them more or less like this:
"We'll see."

Fifteen boys are now living a quiet life.
They have done their heavy chores
of snowdrops, despair and writing letters.
Girls love them—
some more beautiful than me,

иные некрасивее.
Пятнадцать мальчиков преувеличенно свободно, а подчас
            злорадно
приветствуют меня при встрече,
приветствуют во мне при встрече
свое освобожденье, нормальный сон и пищу...

Напрасно ты идешь, последний мальчик.
Поставлю я твои подснежники в стакан,
и коренастые их стебли обрастут
серебряными пузырьками...
Но, видишь ли, и ты меня разлюбишь
и, победив себя, ты будешь говорить со мной надменно,
как будто победил меня,
а я пойду по улице, по улице...

ВУЛКАНЫ

Молчат потухшие вулканы.
На дно их падает зола.
Там отдыхают великаны
после содеянного зла.

Все холоднее их владенья,
все тяжелее их плечам,
но те же грешные виденья
являются им по ночам.

others less beautiful.
Fifteen boys with a show of freedom, and at times spite
salute me when we meet,
salute in me, when we meet,
their liberation, normal sleep and regular meals.

In vain you come to me, last boy.
I shall place your snowdrops in a glass of water,
and silver bubbles will cover
their stocky stems . . .
But, you see, you too will cease to love me,
and, mastering yourself, you'll talk in a superior way,
as though you'd mastered me,
and I'll walk off down the street, down the street . . .

1960

THE VOLCANOES

Extinct volcanoes brood in silence.
Ash scatters down into their keep.
Reposing from their evil deeds,
the giants now are sunk in sleep.

A growing chill pervades their realm.
Their shoulders hunch under the strain.
But, as before, their sinful visions
come haunting them at night again.

Им снится город обреченный,
не знающий своей судьбы,
базальт, в колонны обращенный
и обрамляющий сады.

Там девочки берут в охапки
цветы, что расцвели давно,
там знаки подают вакханки
мужчинам, тянущим вино.

Все разгораясь и глупея,
там пир идет, там речь груба.
О девочка моя, Помпея,
дитя царевны и раба!

В плену судьбы своей везучей
о чем ты думала, о ком,
когда так храбро о Везувий
ты опиралась локотком?

Заслушалась его рассказов,
расширила зрачки свои,
чтобы не вынести раскатов
безудержной его любви.

И он челом своим умнейшим
тогда же, на исходе дня,
припал к ногам твоим умершим
и закричал: «Прости меня!»

They dream of a city doomed to perish
that has no inkling of its fate,
of basalt hardening into columns,
and gardens framed in lava's spate.

Girls fill their arms with flowers there,
flowers that bloomed a time ago.
Bacchantes lure the men who sip
cool wine beneath a portico.

The feast's begun; excitement mounts
and stupifies, and speech grows coarse.
O my lovely girl, Pompeii, child
begotten of a slave and empress!

A captive of your oozy fate,
what were you thinking, and of whom,
when you so bravely leaned upon
Vesuvius for some elbow room.

Rapt by the stories he was telling,
you stared big-eyed in terror,
unable to resist the peals
of his overbearing ardor.

At the close of day, it came about,
he fell and pressed his brightest brow
to your already lifeless feet,
and burst out with: "Forgive me now!"

1962

ЛОДКА

В траве глубоко и сыро,
если шагнуть с крыльца.
Держу я чужого сына,
похожего на отца.

Держу высоко, неловко
и говорю: «Смотри!
Видишь, какая лодка
синяя изнутри!

Возьмем леденцы, орехи,
что у меня в столе.
Посмотрим, какие реки
водятся на земле.

Есть и река смешная.
Она течет далеко.
Наверно, она смешала
воду и молоко.

Сахарных рыб немало
в гуще ее рябой...»
Но бровью поводит мама,
глядя на нас с тобой.

Нам не устроить побега,
речек не увидать.
Сына после обеда
строго уложат спать.

Окна, закройтесь плотно,
лампочка, не гори!
А сыну приснится лодка,
синяя изнутри.

THE BOAT

The grass is deep and damp
when you step off the porch.
I'm holding another's son,
the image of his father.

I hold him clumsily
and high, and say: "Look there!
Do you see the boat
that is all blue inside!

"We'll open my table drawer,
and take some nuts and candy.
Let's go and see what rivers
are to be found on earth.

"There is one funny river.
It flows a long long way.
Most likely it's a mixture
of running milk and water.

"In its swirling depths there is
no lack of sugar fish."
But as they stare at you and me,
your mama's eyebrows twitch.

We can't now run away;
we'll never see those rivers.
The son will be put to bed
most firmly after dinner.

Windows, close up tight!
Lamp, stop burning bright!
And the son will dream of a boat
that is all blue inside.

В тот месяц май, в тот месяц мой
во мне была такая легкость,
и, расстилаясь над землей,
влекла меня погоды летность.

Я так щедра была, щедра
в счастливом предвкушенье пенья,
и с легкомыслием щегла
я окунала в воздух перья.

Но, слава богу, стал мой взор
и проницательней, и строже,
и каждый вздох и каждый взлет
обходится мне все дороже.

И я причастна к тайнам дня.
Открыты мне его явленья.
Вокруг оглядываюсь я
с усмешкой старого еврея.

Я вижу, как грачи галдят,
над черным снегом нависая,
как скучно женщины глядят,
склонившиеся над вязаньем.

И где-то, в дудочку дудя,
не соблюдая клумб и грядок,
чужое бегает дитя
и нарушает их порядок.

IN THAT MONTH OF MAY

In that month of May, that month of mine,
I felt so easy and so light,
and, spreading above the earth,
the flying weather drew me after.

I was so generous, so generous,
in the joyous foretaste of much song,
and as light-headed as a goldfinch,
I dipped my feathers in the air.

But, thank the Lord, my gaze became
more rigorous and penetrating,
and every sigh and every flight
now costs me more and more.

And I'm privy to the secrets of the day . . .
Its phenomena are revealed to me.
Smiling like an old ironic Jew,
I observe what's happening around me.

I see the loudly cawing rooks
above the black snow hanging;
the weary glances of the women
as they stoop above their knitting.

And piping somewhere on a pipe,
unmindful of neat beds of flowers,
a stranger child goes scampering about
and violating their established order.

1962

Не уделяй мне много времени,
вопросов мне не задавай.
Глазами добрыми и верными
руки моей не задевай.

Не проходи весной по лужицам,
по следу следа моего.
Я знаю — снова не получится
из этой встречи ничего.

Ты думаешь, что я из гордости
хожу, с тобою не дружу?
Я не из гордости — из горести
так прямо голову держу.

DON'T GIVE ME ALL OF YOUR TIME

Don't give me all of your time,
don't question me so often.
With eyes so true and faithful
don't try and catch my hands.

Don't follow in the Spring
my steps through pools of rain.
I know that of our meeting
nothing will come again.

You think it's pride that makes
me turn my back on you?
It's grief, not pride that holds
my head so very straight.

1962

ДЕКАБРЬ

Мы соблюдаем правила зимы.
Играем мы, не уступая смеху,
и, придавая очертанья снегу,
приподнимаем белый снег с земли.

И, будто бы предчувствуя беду,
прохожие толпятся у забора,
снедает их тяжелая забота:
а что с тобой имеем мы в виду.

Мы бабу лепим, только и всего.
О, это торжество и удивленье,
когда и высота, и удлиненье
зависят от движенья твоего.

Ты говоришь: — Смотри, как я леплю. —
Действительно, как хорошо ты лепишь
и форму от бесформенности лечишь.
Я говорю: — Смотри, как я люблю.

Снег уточняет все свои черты
и слушается нашего приказа.
И вдруг я замечаю, как прекрасно
лицо, что к снегу обращаешь ты.

Проходим мы по белому двору,
мимо прохожих, с выраженьем дерзким.
С лицом таким же пристальным и детским,
любимый мой, всегда играй в игру.

Поддайся его долгому труду,
о моего любимого работа!
Даруй ему удачливость ребенка,
рисующего домик и трубу.

DECEMBER

We now observe the rules of winter,
and on the snow impose design
and, in play restraining laughter,
we scoop the white snow from the ground.

And then, as if foreseeing ill,
pedestrians crowd about the fence;
an anxious question gnaws at them:
what are they doing, this odd couple?

We're making a snowman—that is all.
We are triumphant and amazed
when tapering height and breadth depend
on every movement that we make.

You say: "Just look how well I mold."
You are so excellent at this—
to formlessness imparting form.
I answer: "Look, how much I love."

Obedient to our least command,
snow gives precision to your features.
I then detect the beauty of
your face as you bend to the snow.

Past all these people then we stride
out of the snow, our eyes defiant.
When playing games, my love, your features
should always be as childlike and intent.

To his continued labor try to yield,
O work that my beloved does!
Grant him the fluency of a child
who draws a chimney and a house.

1962

BULAT OKUDZHAVA

1924–

Bulat Okudzhava—the name suggests Georgian origin, but the poet was born in Moscow. He is certainly one of the most refreshing literary phenomena of the past decade. Okudzhava is a poet-song writer who usually accompanies his recitation on the guitar. He has a sensitive ear not only to music but to what people are feeling and thinking. Though he writes many simple lyrics, his work may be said to be growing more complex. His frankness and sincerity have on occasions proved disturbing to the dogmatists. And his prose stories—those about the war in which he was wounded—eschew the official heroic attitudes and are full of frank and subtle realism. Despite occasional obstacles, Okudzhava has gradually managed to get into the literary magazines of the 1960's. His first two books were *Lyrics* (1956) and *Islands* (1959). His later poetry, however, shows considerable technical and thematic development.

World War II found Okudzhava in Moscow. In 1942, he volunteered and fought at the front. In 1950 he finished the Tbilisi State University. After teaching for a time in a village school, he returned to Moscow where he now works. His poetry is now often printed in *Yunost, Molodaya Gvardia*, and other Soviet magazines. He also takes part in public poetry readings together with Yevtushenko and Voznesensky.

ДЕТСТВО

Синело утро. Было рано.
Москва измученно спала.
Вдруг в окна
           сквозь двойные рамы
послышались колокола.

И я взглянул на небо в страхе:
там,
      сквозь туман,
              издалека
ломились черные монахи...
А это были облака.

Колокола. Мороз по коже.
Горели грешники в аду.
И где-то мыкался прохожий
у Саваофа на виду.

...Я был послушный и неслышный.
Про Бога нянька мне врала.
Грозилась чертом и Всевышним
и в церковь кланяться звала.

Да, знать, врала она без меры,
переборщила сгоряча...
...Шли по Арбату пионеры,
шли, в барабаны грохоча,

и что-то пели про картошку,
про пионерскую еду,
и я глядел на них в окошко
у Саваофа на виду.

CHILDHOOD

Blue was the morning. It was early yet.
Tormented Moscow was still sleeping.
Through the windows,
                                through the double panes,
Bells suddenly could be heard ringing.

And glancing at the sky in fear,
I saw,
        through the mist there
                                    from afar,
black monks jostling their way . . .
Those were the clouds.

Ding dong. Ding dong. Frost chills the skin.
Sinners were burning in hell.
And a pedestrian somewhere was dawdling
in plain view of Sabaoth.

I was abashed and barely audible.
My nanny lied about God.
She threatened me with the Almighty and the devil
and bid me go to church and humble myself.

Yes, she lied extravagantly,
and piled it on in her zeal . . .
Along the Arbat pioneers were marching,
marching with drums beating.

And they were singing about the potato,
their staple pioneer diet.
And I stared at them from the window
in plain view of Sabaoth.

А Бог мигнул мне глазом черным
так, ни с того и ни с сего,
и вдруг я понял: это ж дворник
стоит у дома моего.

БАЛЛАДА О ДОНКИХОТАХ

У Москвы у реки, в переулке Глубоком,
дульцинеи взирают из окон,
ждут, когда возвратятся с работы
донкихоты,
и на синем огне из веселой крупы
сочиняют супы.
Их немного состарило время — века и заботы,
но...
идут донкихоты.
Вот они поднимаются постепенно
на свои этажи, на свои чердаки,
и гремят каблуки по ступеням,
и поют соловьями звонки.
Дульцинея, встречай!
Вот он входит усталым шагом
с краснопресненскими ландышами в руке,
не в доспехах и не со шпагой,
а в рабочем своем пиджаке.
Дульцинея,
а помнишь своего Дон-Кихота
в минувшие года?
Дульцинея,
а помнишь: уходила пехота

And God winked at me with his black eye
out of the blue, so to speak,
and all at once I was aware of the janitor
standing there, just outside my house.

BALLAD ABOUT DON QUIXOTES

By the Moscow River, in Gluboki Street,
Dulcineas peer from windows,
waiting for their Don Quixotes to return
from work,
and from bubbling barley
they compose soups on a blue flame.
Time's aged them slightly—cares weigh on their eyelids,
but . . .
the Don Quixotes are coming.
Step by step they walk up
to their floors, their attics,
and their heels thud on the stairs
and doorbells sound like nightingales.
Welcome them, Dulcinea!
He enters now with tired step
holding a bunch of lily-of-the-valley,
clad in no armor, carrying no sword,
wearing a plain working jacket.
Dulcinea,
do you remember your Don Quixote
of yesteryears?
Dulcinea,
do you remember the infantry

неведомо куда,
где того и гляди
встретит смерть на пути,
стукнет пуля в висок
наискосок,
и смолкнет скучный ее голосок...
А рыцарский скарб — по музеям весь:
стали музеям мечи ценнее,
но
гранату за пояс, винтовку наперевес
и
«Ты не плачь, я вернусь, Дульцинея!»

...Да, живут донкихоты!
Я касаюсь в толпе их руки.
Да, я слышу — с рассветом
гремят башмаки вдоль реки.
Да, взирают из окон,
да, глядят,
как над городом вечер синеет
нежданный...
В переулке Голубом,
как столетья назад,
дульцинеи
жаждут
свиданий.

as it went off, destination unknown,
where, at any moment,
death will meet them on the way,
a bullet obliquely strike
a temple,
and its droning voice be heard no more.
The panoply of knighthood is all in the museums:
museums attach increasing value on swords,
but
stick a grenade in your belt, hold your rifle atilt,
and
"Don't weep, Dulcinea, I'll be back!"

. . . Yes, there are Don Quixotes still alive!
In any crowd I brush against their hands.
Yes, at dawn I hear
boots thudding on the riverside.
Yes, they gaze from windows,
yes, they watch
the blue glow of unexpected evening
above the town.
In Gluboki Street,
as in centuries past,
Dulcineas
yearn for
a lover's tryst.

ЧЕЛОВЕК

Дышет воздухом, дышет первой травой,
камышем, пока он колышется,
всякой песенкой, пока она слышится,
теплой ладонью под головой.
Дышет, дышет — никак не надышется.

Дышет матерью —
                она у него одна,
дышет родиной —
                она у него единственная,
плачет, мучается, смеется, посвистывает
и молчит у окна, и поет дотемна,
и влюбленно недолгий свой век перелистывает.

MAN

He breathes in the air, breathes in the early grass,
breathes the rushes while they stir,
every song while it can still be heard,
a warm woman's hand cupped beneath his head.
Breathes, breathes—but cannot breathe enough.

Breathes his mother—
                    she who is the only one.
Breathes his country—
                    he has no other.
Weeps, suffers, laughs, whistles,
and stands silent at the window, and sings till dusk,
and lovingly leafs through his brief life.

Один солдат на свете жил,
красивый и отважный,
но он игрушкой детской был, —
ведь был солдат бумажный.

Он переделать мир хотел,
чтоб был счастливым каждый,
но над кроваткой все висел, —
ведь был солдат бумажный.

Он был бы рад в огонь и в дым,
за вас погибнуть дважды,
но потешались вы над ним, —
ведь был солдат бумажный.

Не поверяли вы ему
своих секретов важных.
А почему? а потому,
что был солдат бумажный.

А он, судьбу свою кляня,
не тихой жизни жаждал
и всё просил: — Огня, огня! —
забыв, что он бумажный.

В огонь? Ну, что ж. Иди! Идешь?
И он шагнул отважно.
И там погиб он ни за грош, —
ведь был солдат бумажный.

A PAPER SOLDIER

In our world there lived a soldier.
He was extremely handsome, very brave,
but he happened to be a children's toy—
for he was merely a paper soldier.

He wished to refashion all the world,
to make each individual happy,
but he dangled over a child's cot,
for he was merely a paper soldier.

He would have dashed through smoke and fire,
and given his life for you twice over,
but you only derided him and laughed—
for he was merely a paper soldier.

You were unwilling to entrust
him with your most important secrets.
And why did you not trust him? Oh, just
because he was a paper soldier.

And kicking against his wretched lot,
he thirsted for a life less tranquil,
and kept demanding: "Fire! Yes, Fire!"
forgetting he was a paper soldier.

Into fire? All right. Why not plunge in?
And bravely forward he marched off.
And there he perished, nothing won—
for he was merely a paper soldier.

1960

ЭХ ТЫ, ШАРИК ГОЛУБОЙ

Эх ты, шарик голубой,
Грустная планета!
Что ж мы делаем с тобой?
Для чего всё это?
Все мы топчемся в крови,
А ведь мы могли бы...

Реки, полные любви,
По тебе текли бы!

ЭТО СЛУЧИТСЯ

Это случится, случится,
этого не миновать:
вскрикнут над городом птицы,
будут оркестры играть,
станет прозрачнее воздух,
пушек забудется гам,
и пограничное войско
с песней уйдет по домам.
Это случится, случится —
верю: расплавят броню...
Не забывайте учиться
этому нужному дню!

AH, YOU AZURE GLOBULE

Ah, you azure globule,
planet very sad.
You and I, what's doing?
What's it all about?
We all squelch through gore
instead of doing more . . .

Rivers brimmed with love
over you might flow.

THIS WILL HAPPEN

This will happen, happen,
no way of avoiding this:
the birds will shrill above the town,
orchestras will play,
the air will grow more limpid,
the guns' thud will be forgotten,
and the army of the frontier
will march home singing.
This will happen, happen—
I believe they'll smelt the armor . . .
Don't forget to learn
from this essential day . . .

1963

Вся земля, вся планета —
сплошное туда...
Как струна, дорога
звонка и туга.
Все куда бы ни ехали —
только туда,
и никто не сюда —
все туда и туда.

Остаюсь я один,
вот так остаюсь.
И боюсь, и признаться боюсь,
что боюсь.
Сам себя осуждаю, корю и курю.
Вдруг какая-то женщина — сердце горит.
— Вы куда? — удивленно я ей говорю.
— Я сюда, — так влюбленно она говорит.
Сумасшедшая, — думаю, — вот ерунда!
Как же можно сюда,
Когда нужно туда?

ALL THE EARTH

All the earth, the whole planet,
is one big rush over there . . .
The road's as taut
and vibrant as a string.
Wherever they may go, all
are bent on going there,
and no one comes this way,
but always over there, there.

I'm left here all alone,
left simply alone.
And I am frightened, and fear
to admit my fear.
I condemn myself, heap blame on blame.
Of a sudden a woman—my heart's on fire.
"Where are you going?" I ask in surprise.
"This way," very lovingly she replies.
"She's mad," I think. "It makes no sense!"
How can she be coming here,
when she ought to be going there?

Берегите нас, поэтов, берегите нас.
Остается век, полвека, год, неделя, час,
три минуты, две минуты, вовсе ничего...
Берегите нас, но только — все за одного.

Берегите нас с грехами, с радостью и без...
Где-то юный и прекрасный бродит наш Дантес.
Он минувшее проклятье не успел забыть,
но велит ему призванье пулю в ствол забить.

Где-то плачет наш Мартынов, поминает кровь.
Он уже убил однажды, он не хочет вновь,
но судьба его такая, и свинец отлит.
И двадцатое столетье так ему велит.

Берегите нас покуда можно уберечь.
Только так не берегите, чтоб костьми нам лечь.
Только так не берегите, как борзых — псари,
только так не берегите, как псарей — цари.

Берегите нас, поэтов, от дурацких рук,
от нелепых приговоров, от слепых подруг.
Будут вам стихи и песни, и еще не раз.
Только вы нас берегите, берегите нас.

PROTECT US POETS

Protect us poets, and guard us well.
What's left?—a century, a year, a week,
An hour, three minutes, two, nothing at all . . .
Protect us, but only if all support the one.

Protect us though we sin, have joy or none.
Our D'Anthès walks somewhere, young and handsome.
He's had no time to forget his ancient curse,
And his vocation bids him load his pistol.

Somewhere our Martynov weeps, recalling blood.
He has killed, but hesitates to slay again;
Yet, that's his fate, and the bullet's cast.
The age we live in prompts him to the act.

Protect us while you still are able.
But don't guard as you would a sack of bones.
Don't cherish us as huntsmen cherish hounds.
Don't cherish us the way Tsars cherish huntsmen.

Protect us poets from all foolish hands,
From stupid judgments and near-sighted girls.
We'll give you songs and poems—more than one.
Protect us then, and guard us well.

Не верь войне, мальчишка,
не верь, она грустна,
она грустна, мальчишка,
как сапоги тесна.

Твои лихие кони
не смогут ничего,
ты весь, как на ладони,
все пули — в одного.

DON'T BELIEVE IN WAR

Don't believe in war, my boy,
don't believe, it's quite depressing,
it's as depressing, boy,
as a pair of boots that pinch.

Those swift romantic steeds of yours,
they are good for nothing here;
you're as exposed as an open palm,
and the bullets' only target.

ЛЕНИНГРАДСКАЯ МУЗЫКА

Пока еще звезды последние не отгорели,
вы встаньте, вы встаньте с постели,
сойдите к дворам,
туда,
где дрова, словно крылья
лесной акварели...
И тихая скрипка Растрелли
послышится вам.
Неправда, неправда, всё враки,
что будто бы старят
старанья и годы!
Едва вы окажетесь тут,
как в колокола
купола золотые ударят,
колонны
горластые трубы свои задерут.
Веселую полночь люби, да на утро
надейся...
Когда ни грехов и ни горестей
не отмолить,
танцуя,
игла опрокинется с Адмиралтейства
и в сердце ударит, чтоб сонную кровь отворить.
О, вовсе не ради парада, не ради награды,
а только для нас,
выходящих с зарей из ворот,
гремят барабаны гранита,
кларнеты ограды
свистят менуэты...
И улица Росси поет.

LENINGRAD MUSIC

While the last stars have not yet burned out,
rise up, rise up out of bed,
　　　　　go down into the courtyards,
where
　　　stacks of logs look like the wings
　　　　　　　of a woodland aquarelle.
And you will hear
　　　　Rastrelli's gentle violin.
It's untrue, untrue, all lies,
　　　　when they maintain
that striving and years make you old!
　　　　As soon as you get down here,
the cupolas of gold
　　　will boom with bells,
the columns
　　　　　will raise their trumpets.
Love the glad midnight, have hope
　　　　　　　for tomorrow . . .
When prayer can allay
　　　　　neither sin nor sorrow,
the dancing
Admiralty needle will fall
and transfix your heart, forcing your drowsy blood.
Oh, not for parade, not for any reward,
but only for our sake,
　　　　as we step out of the gates with the dawn,
will the drums of granite roll,
the clarinets of the railings
　　　　　　　whistle menuets . . .
And Rossi's street sings songs.

VICTOR SOSNORA

1937–

Victor Sosnora is gradually beginning to emerge as one of the more interesting poets of the 1960's. He lives and publishes mainly in Leningrad. His first book, *The January Shower*, appeared in 1962; another volume, *Triptych*, in 1965. A factory worker, he has only recently become a member of the Writers' Union in Leningrad. Very little of his poetry has been printed in the big magazines. He has been criticized for obscurity and for showing the influence of such poets as Khlebnikov, Severyanin and Pasternak. Sosnora is essentially a poet who works in images and loves to create subtle and complex verbal rhythms and associations. His language is recherché and he sometimes uses archaic words. His poetry is dense and some of his effects can only be described as surrealistic. It also has a pronounced musical quality.

А ели звенели металлом зеленым!

Их зори лизали!
Морозы вонзались!
А ели звенели металлом зеленым!
Коньками по наледи!
Гонгом вокзальным!

Был купол у каждой из елей заломлен,
как шлем металлурга,
как замок над валом!
Хоть ели звенели металлом зеленым,
я знал достоверно:
они деревянны.

Они, насажденья зеленые,
                              стынут
любым миллиграммом своей протоплазмы,
они — теплотворны,
они — сердцевинны
и ждут не дождутся:
а может быть — праздник?

ПОЛНОЧЬ

А тени возле зданий,
тени —
прочерченные криво
грани.

AND FIR TREES CLANGED

And fir trees clanged in green metal!

The early dawns licked them!
The frosts stabbed into them!
And the fir trees clanged in green metal!
Like skates scraping on ice!
Like a railway station gong!

The cupola of each fir was bent back
like an iron worker's helmet,
like a castle perched above a rampart!
Though the fir trees clanged in green metal,
I knew for certain
they were wooden.

They, the green plantations,
                                    are freezing
in every milligram of their protoplasm;
they are califerous,
they're full of pith,
and on tenterhooks:
perhaps—it's a holiday?

1964

MIDNIGHT

And the shadows by the buildings
the shadows—
their edges
crookedly drawn.

Взгляни туда-сюда:
антенны —
завинченные в крыши
грабли.

Сырая колабаха
ветер!
А дворников берет
зевота.
Как плети Карабаса,
ветви.
И все наоборот
сегодня.

Луна,
а на граните
сухо.
Волна —
              невпроворот! —
лучится.
Бывает: на границе
суток
все ждешь: наоборот
случится.

Вороны как барбосы
лают,
и каркают собаки
грозно.
Ты ничего не бойся,
лада.
Все это — байки.

Просто — проза
моих сомнений.
Соль на марле!
К утру мои просохнут
весла.

Glance here and there:
antennae—
                    rakes
screwed into roofs.

The wind's
a sodden hunk of bread!
and the janitors
start yawning.
The branches
are like the whips of Carabas.
And everything
today is topsy-turvy.

The moon is out,
and yet the granite's
dull.
By contrast,
                    a wave
is shining.
It can happen
that the opposite will come to pass
as we wait on the brink
of the next twenty-four hours.

The ravens bark
like a big shaggy dog,
and dogs croak
in a threatening way.
Don't let this frighten you,
my lovely.
It's all fantastic tales.

Simply—the prose
of my doubts.
Salt-sprinkled gauze!
By morning
my oars will dry.

И утром будет все
нормально,
как все, что утром,
все,
        что звездно!

ГОЛОЛЕДИЦА

А вчера еще,
                вчера
снег выкидывал коленца.
Нынче улица черна —
го-ло-ле-дица.
На морозе башмаки
восторженно каркают:
это ходят рыбаки
по зеркальным карпам.
От меня блестит заря!
И прокатные станы!
Это ходят слесаря
по легированной стали!
Дети ходят в Летний сад
по леденцам!
И сулит король-обманщик
бесчисленные горы.

Но когда-то крикнет мальчик,
что король-то
                голый!

And by morning all
will be normal,
like everything in the morning,
everything
                starlit!

1964

SHARP FROST

And yesterday still,
                    yesterday,
the snow was playing tricks.
Now the street is black—
sharp frost—sheet ice.
In the frost with exultation
boots croak out:
it is the fishermen tramping
on glassy carp.
Out of me shines a red glow!
And a rolling-mill!
It is the locksmiths trampling
on alloyed steel!
Children walk on glazed sugar-candy
to the Summer Garden!
And the king-the-cheat holds out
the promise of countless mountains.

But one day the boy will cry out:
The king
        is naked!

1965

ANDREY VOZNESENSKY

1933–

With his third book of poems, *The Triangular Pear* (1962), Andrey Voznesensky has shown himself a master of complex forms and varied rhythms. Some of his later poems mix classical stanzas with passages of rhythmical prose. In addition he has been elaborating a new vocabulary, which shows his awareness and poetic use of technical terms drawn from the fields of science and modern technique. In other poems, he demonstrates a developing sense of history and its particular terminology, including an occasional but appropriate use of archaic, technical or historical words. Voznesensky now gives the impression of being a poet who is striving after a modern synthesis of past and present. Voznesensky also shows himself well acquainted with the modernist experiments of the Russian Futurist poets such as Mayakovsky and he has a keen ear for Pasternak's early rhythms. He also knows the work of the Western poets such as Apollinaire, Paul Eluard and Garcia Lorca. He tends to work in images, and has a strong visual sense. At times a note of irony intrudes as in "Antiworlds" and "Six Strophes." But even in his "mixed" poems there is always room for lyrical passages. He also continues to write poems of pure lyrical feeling ("Arrested Motion," for example). When these are compared with the earlier lyrical poems of his first book, *Mosaica* (1960), which were only deceptively simple, it becomes clear that Voznesensky has considerably enriched his language, sense of form and subtle power of expression.

Andrey Voznesensky was born in Moscow. He studied to become an architect and then took up poetry as a full time profession. He had begun appearing in print in 1958. He has since traveled to the United States, France, England, and Italy. He was under a cloud for a time in 1963, but has resumed his poetic excursions since 1964. He has visited the United States for a second time in 1966 on a reading tour.

Сидишь беременная, бледная.
Как ты переменилась, бедная.

Сидишь, одергиваешь платьице,
И плачется тебе, и плачется...

За что нас только бабы балуют
И губы, падая, дают,

И выбегают за шлагбаумы,
И от вагонов отстают?

Как ты бежала за вагонами,
Глядела в полосы оконные...

Стучат почтовые, курьерские,
Хабаровские, люберецкие...

И от Москвы до Ашхабада,
Остолбенев до немоты,

Стоят, как каменные, бабы,
Луне подставив животы.

И, поворачиваясь к свету,
В ночном быту необжитом —

Как понимает их планета
Своим огромным животом.

PREGNANT YOU SIT

Pregnant you sit, and pale.
How you have changed, poor girl.

Plucking at your dress, you sit
And want to weep and weep . . .

What makes you women spoil us
And, falling, yield your lips,

Then run beyond the stations,
Outstripped by speeding trains . . .

How hard you tried to keep up
With the blurring carriage windows . . .

Trains rattle by, express and mail,
Trains to Khabarovsk and elsewhere . . .

From Moscow all the way
To Ashkabad, like numb idols,

Women stand as if turned to stone,
Their bellies proferred to the moon.

And swinging into the light
Of the unpeopled life of the night—

How well the moon, with her
Big belly, understands them.

1958

ПЕРВЫЙ ЛЕД

Мерзнет девочка в автомате,
Прячет в зябкое пальтецо
Все в слезах и губной помаде
Перемазанное лицо.

Дышит в худенькие ладошки.
Пальцы — льдышки. В ушах — сережки.

Ей обратно одной, одной
Вдоль по улочке ледяной.

Первый лед. Это в первый раз.
Первый лед телефонных фраз.

Мерзлый след на щеках блестит —
Первый лед от людских обид.

FIRST ICE

A girl freezes in a telephone booth.
In her draughty overcoat she hides
A face all smeared
In tears and lipstick.

She breathes on her thin palms.
Her fingers are icicles. She wears earrings.

She'll have to walk home alone, alone,
Along the ice-bound street.

First ice. The very first time.
The first ice of telephone phrases.

Frozen tears glisten on her cheeks—
The first ice of human hurt.

1958 [1960]

СВАДЬБА

Выходит замуж молодость
Не за кого — за что.
Себя ломает молодость
За модное манто.

За золотые горы
И в серебре виски.
Эх, да по фарфору
Ходят сапоги!

Где пьют, там и бьют —
Чашки, кружки об пол бьют.
Горшки — в черепки,
Молодым под каблуки.
Брызжут чашки на куски:
Чье-то счастье —
В черепки!

И ты в прозрачной юбочке,
Юна, бела,
Дрожишь, как будто рюмочка
На краешке стола.

Улыбочка, как трещинка,
Играет на губах,
И мокрые отметинки
Темнеют на щеках.

Где пьют, там и льют —
Слезы, слезы, слезы льют...

WEDDING

Young girls get married, marry
Not someone but some thing.
Youth will fidget and strain
After a fashionable coat.

After the golden mountains
And curls pinned up in silver.
And oh! boots go trampling on
The finest porcelain.

Where people drink, they smash things,
Smash cups and mugs to the floor;
Under the young men's heels
Pots break to smithereens.
Cups splash to bits:
A person's happiness
Is shattered into shards.

And you in the transparent skirt,
So young and milk-white,
You quiver like a glass
Set on the edge of a table.

A smile like a small crack
Plays on your lips.
And little tears have left
Dark smudges on your cheeks . . .

Where people drink, they spill,
Tears, tears, tears, spill, spill . . .

1959 [*1964*]

ТАЙГА

Твои зубы смелы.
В них усмешка ножа.
И гудят, как шмели,
Золотые глаза!

Мы бредем от избушки.
Нам трава до ушей.
Ты пророчишь мне взбучку
От родных и друзей.

Ты отнюдь не монахиня,
Хоть в округе — скиты.
Бродят пчелы мохнатые,
Нагибая цветы.

Я не знаю — тайги.
Я не знаю — семьи.
Знаю только зрачки.
Знаю — зубы твои.

На ромашках роса,
Как в буддийских пиалах.
Как она хороша
В длинных мочках фиалок!

В каждой капельке-мочке,
Отражаясь, нагая,
Ты дрожишь, как Дюймовочка,
Лепестки нагибая.

Ты — живая вода
На губах, на листке.
Ты себя раздала
Всю до капли — тайге.

TAIGA

You have such bold teeth,
And a knife of a smile.
And the gold of your eyes
Hums like a flight of hornets.

We stroll away from the hut,
Up to our ears in grass.
My parents and friends, you predict,
Will haul me over the coals.

But you're hardly a nun
Even among hermit retreats.
Furry bees wander here,
Bending the flowers.

I don't know the taiga.
I don't know my parents.
I only know your pupils.
I know—your teeth.

The dew on the daisies
Glistens as in a Buddhist bowl.
How lovely she looks in
The long fibrils of cyclamen.

In every drop on each fibril,
Reflected there, naked,
You quiver, Minute One,
Bending the petals.

You are the living water
On the lips, on a leaf.
To the last drop—you have given
The taiga all of yourself.

1960

ПАРАБОЛИЧЕСКАЯ БАЛЛАДА

Судьба, как ракета, летит по параболе
Обычно — во мраке и реже — по радуге.

Жил огненно-рыжий художник Гоген,
Богема, а в прошлом — торговый агент.
Чтоб в Лувр королевский попасть
                                        из Монмартра,
Он
      дал
            кругаля через Яву с Суматрой!

Унесся, забыв сумасшествие денег,
Кудахтанье жен, духоту академий.
Он преодолел
                  тяготенье земное.

Жрецы гоготали за кружкой пивною:
«Прямая — короче, парабола — круче,
Не лучше ль скопировать райские кущи?»

А он уносился ракетой ревущей
Сквозь ветер, срывающий фалды и уши.
И в Лувр он попал не сквозь главный порог —
Параболой
              гневно
                      пробив потолок!

Идут к своим правдам, по-разному храбро,
Червяк — через щель, человек — по параболе.

Жила-была девочка рядом в квартале.
Мы с нею учились, зачеты сдавали.
Куда ж я уехал!
                    И черт меня нес
Меж грузных тбилисских двусмысленных звезд!

PARABOLIC BALLAD

Fate-the-rocket described a parabola
In darkness mostly, more rarely on a rainbow.

Fiery-haired Gauguin the painter lived
As a bohemian, though once he'd been a stockbroker.
To get into the royal Louvre
                    from Montmartre,
He
    turned
            a somersault through Java and Sumatra!

He rushed off, forgetting the craze for money,
the clucking wives, the stale air of Academies.
He conquered
            the gravity of earth.

The augurs guffawed over their steins of beer:
"A straight line is shorter, a parabola steeper.
Isn't it better to copy the groves of paradise?"

And he sped away, a roaring rocket,
Through the wind that ripped off coat-tails and ears.
And he landed in the Louvre, through no main entrance
But in a parabola
                fiercely
                        smashing through the ceiling!

Bravely each man in his fashion seeks the truth:
A worm crawling through a crack, man in a parabola.

There was a girl who lived in my quarter.
We attended school together, sent in our term papers.
Where had I gone?!
                    And the devil made off with me
In between the ponderous, ambiguous stars of Tbilisi!

Прости мне дурацкую эту параболу.
Простывшие плечики в черном парадном...
О, как ты звенела во мраке Вселенной
Упруго и прямо — как прутик антенны!
А я все лечу,

                   приземляясь по ним —
Земным и озябшим твоим позывным.
Как трудно дается нам эта парабола!..

Сметая каноны, прогнозы, параграфы,
Несутся искусство,

                   любовь

                          и история —
По параболической траектории!

В сибирской весне утопают калоши

. . . .
А может быть, все же прямая — короче?

Please forgive me this foolish parabola.
Those frail shivering shoulders in best evening black . . .
O how you rang out to me in the black Universe,
Direct and resilient—like the rod of an antenna!
But I was still flying,

                    getting my bearings to land
From your earthly, chilled, persistent summonses.
How hard it is for us to execute this parabola! . . .

Sweeping aside canons, prognoses, paragraphs,
Art,

     love

        and history speed
In a parabolic trajectory!

Galoshes sink in the Siberian spring
. . . .
Perhaps the straight line is shorter after all?

1959 [1960]

ГОЙЯ

Я — Гойя!
Глазницы воронок мне выклевал ворог,
                                                слетая на поле нагое.
Я — горе.

Я — голос.
Войны, городов головни
                                        на снегу сорок первого года.
Я — голод.

Я — горло
Повешенной бабы, чье тело, как колокол,
                                        било над площадью голой...
Я — Гойя!

О грозди
Возмездья! Взвил залпом на Запад —
                                        я пепел незваного гостя!
И в мемориальное небо вбил крепкие звезды —
Как гвозди.

Я — Гойя.

GOYA

I am Goya!
Swooping down on a bare field,
                        a foe pecked craters in my eyes.
I am grief.

I am the groan
Of war, the charred guts of cities
                        in the snow of 'forty-one.
I am hunger.

I am the gasp
     Of a hanged woman, whose body clanged like a bell
                        above the naked square . . .

I am Goya!

O grapes
Of wrath! Westward in a salvo I raised
                        the ash of the intruder!
And in the memorial sky I hammered stars
Firm as nails.

I am Goya!

1960

ВТОРОЕ ПОСВЯЩЕНИЕ

Москва бурлит, как варево,
Под колокольный звон...

Вам,
Варвары
Всех времен!

Цари, тираны,
В тиарах яйцевидных,
В пожарищах-сутанах
И с жерлами цилиндров!

Империи и кассы
Страхуя от огня,
Вы видели в Пегасе
Троянского коня.

Ваш враг — резец и кельма.
И выжженные очи,
Как
Клейма,
Горели среди ночи.

Вас мое слово судит.
Да будет — срам,
Да
Будет
Проклятье вам!

SECOND DEDICATION

Beneath the booming bells,
Moscow is seething like a brew . . .

To you,
Barbarians
Of all times!

Tsars, tyrants,
In egg-shaped crowns,
In robes of flaming fire,
And with the muzzles of your tophats!

Empires and insurance brokers
Insuring against fire,
In Pegasus you saw
A Trojan horse.

Your enemy's the chisel and the trowel.
And eyes seared out
Burn
Like
Stigmata in the night.

My word condemns you.
May shame be yours,
Shame
And
Damnation too!

1960

АНТИМИРЫ

Живет у нас сосед Букашкин,
Бухгалтер цвета промокашки.
Но, как воздушные шары,
Над ним горят

              Антимиры!

И в них магический, как демон,
Вселенной правит, возлежит
Антибукашкин, академик,
И щупает Лоллобриджид.

Но грезятся Антибукашкину
Виденья цвета промокашки.

Да здравствуют Антимиры!
Фантасты — посреди муры.
Без глупых не было бы умных,
Оазисов — без Каракумов.

Нет женщин —

           есть антимужчины.

В лесах ревут антимашины.
Есть соль земли. Есть сор земли.
Но сохнет сокол без змеи.

Люблю я критиков моих.
На шее одного из них,
Благоуханна и гола,
Сияет антиголова!..

ANTIWORLDS

In our house lives Bukashkin, a neighbor,
a book-keeper, the mat hue of blotting paper,
but above him antiworlds
glow
      like balloons!

But governing the universe in them,
like a demon-magician, reclines
Antibukashkin, academician,
his hands pawing Lollabrigidas.

But before Bukashkin loom
visions the mat hue of blotting paper.

Hail to you, Antiworlds!
Fantasts in a world of slime.
There'd be no clever men without fools.
No oases without the deserts of Karakoum.

There are no women—
                  only antimen.

Antimachines howl in the forests.
The salt of the earth. Earth's garbage too.
But a falcon droops for lack of snakes.

I love my critics.
On the bare and fragrant
Neck of one of them
Shines an antihead! . . .

...Я сплю с окошками открытыми,
А где-то свищет звездопад,
И небоскребы
                   сталактитами
На брюхе глобуса висят.

И подо мной
                   вниз головой,
Вонзившись вилкой в шар земной,
Беспечный, милый мотылек,
Живешь ты,
                   мой антимирок!

Зачем среди ночной поры
Встречаются антимиры?

Зачем они вдвоем сидят
И в телевизоры глядят?

Им не понять и пары фраз.
Их первый раз — последний раз!

Сидят, забывши про бонтон,
Ведь будут мучиться потом!

И ушки красные горят,
Как будто бабочки сидят...

...Знакомый лектор мне вчера
Сказал: «Антимиры? Мура!»
Я сплю, ворочаюсь спросонок.
Наверно, прав научный хмырь...

Мой кот, как радиоприемник,
Зеленым глазом ловит мир.

. . . I sleep with windows open,
And somewhere a starfall whizzes.
And the skyscrapers,

                like stalactites,

hang on the belly of the globe.

And beneath me,

             head down,

Thrust like a fork into the globe,
You live heedless,

             darling moth,

                    my little antiworld!

Why do we come across
The antiworlds at nighttime?

Why do they sit in couples there,
Glued to the television sets?

They can't even catch a pair of phrases.
Their first occasion is their last!

They sit there, forgetting their *bon ton*;
It will make them suffer later on!

And their ears are flaming red,
And they look like butterflies . . .

. . . A lecturer I know said
Yesterday: "Antiworlds! What rot!"
Half-awake, I turn and toss in sleep:
He must be right, that learned dolt . . .
Like a radio, my cat
Snatches at the world with his green eye.

1961 [*1962, 1964*]

ВСТУПИТЕЛЬНОЕ

Открывайся, Америка!
Эврика!

Короную Емельку,
                    открываю, сопя,
В Америке — Америку,
В себе —
         себя.

Рву кожуру с планеты,
                    сметаю пыль и тлен,
Спускаюсь
         в глубь
              предмета,
Как в метрополитен.

Там груши — треугольные,
                    ищу в них души голые.
Я плод трапециевидный
                    беру не чтоб глотать —

Чтоб стекла сердцевинки
Сияли, как алтарь!

Исследуйте, орудуйте,
                    не дуйте в ус,
Пусть врут, что изумрудный, —
Он красный, ваш арбуз!

Вгрызаюсь, как легавая,
                    врубаюсь, как колун...
Художник хулиганит?
Балуй,
      Колумб!

INTRODUCTORY

Open up, America!
Eureka!

I exalt what is common.
                    I discover, wheezing,
In America—America.
Me—
      in myself.

Wrenching off the earth's skin,
                        I brush away dust and mold,
Plunge
      into the depths
             of the subject,
As into a subway.

There I find triangular pears,
                    seek in them bare angular souls.
I take the trapezoid fruit,
              not to swallow it,
But to make the glass of the core
Shine like an altar!

Search, get things done,
                  don't twiddle your thumbs.
Let them pretend it's an emerald—
It's real red, bright red, your watermelon.

I bite into it like a setter,
               cleave deep as an axe . . .
Is the artist behaving like a hooligan?
Play along with me,
           Columbus!

По наитию
          дую к берегу...
Ищешь
       Индию —
Найдешь
       Америку!

НЬЮ-ЙОРКСКАЯ ПТИЦА

На окно ко мне садится
в лунных вензелях
алюминиевая птица —
вместо тела
        фюзеляж

и над ее шеей гайковой
как пламени язык
над гигантской зажигалкой
полыхает
        женский
          лик!

(В простынь капиталистическую
Завернувшись, спит мой друг).

Кто ты? бред кибернетический?
полуробот? полудух?
помесь королевы блюза
и летающего блюдца?

My sixth sense
                    blows me to shore . . .
Bound
        for the Indies,
You discover
                America!

1962

NEW YORK BIRD

Garlanded with moonbeams
an aluminum bird—
                    with fuselage
                                body—
alights on my window,

and above her screw-neck,
a woman's
            face
                flares
like a tongue of flame
over a gigantic lighter!

(Tucked in a capitalist sheet,
My friend is sound asleep.)

who are you? cybernetic delirium?
half-robot? half-spirit?
an amalgam of a queen of the blues
and a flying saucer?

может ты душа Америки
уставшей от забав?
кто ты юная химера
с сигареткою в зубах?

но взирают не мигая
не отерши крем ночной
очи как на Мичигане
у одной

у нее такие газовые
под глазами синячки
птица что предсказываешь?
птица не солги!

что ты знаешь, сообщаешь?
что-то странное извне
как в сосуде сообщающемся
подымается во мне

век атомный стонет в спальне...
(Я ору. И, матерясь,
Мой напарник, как ошпаренный,
Садится на матрас).

America's soul, perhaps,
weary of all the fun?
who are you, teenage chimera,
a cigarette stuck in your teeth?

but they stare unblinking—
the night cream not wiped off—
those eyes like a certain girl's
on Lake Michigan.

she has such gaseous bags
under her eyes.
bird, what do you prophesy?
tell me no lies now, bird!

what do you know, what are you telling?
something strange from the outside
surges up in me
as in a connecting vessel

the atomic age moans in the bedroom . . .
(I yell. And, swearing
As if scalded, my room-mate
Sits up on the mattress.)

1962

МОНОЛОГ БИТНИКА

Э. Неизвестному

Бегите — в себя, на Гаити, в костелы,
                    в клозеты, в Египты —
Бегите!

Нас темные, как Батыи,
Машины поработили.

В судах их клевреты наглые,
Из рюмок дуя бензин,
Вычисляют: кто это в Англии
Вел бунт против машин?
Бежим!..

А в ночь, поборовши робость,
Создателю своему
Кибернетический робот:

«Отдай, — говорит, — жену!
Имею слабость к брюнеткам, — говорит. —
                                        Люблю
на тридцати оборотах. Лучше по-хорошему
                                    уступите!..»

О хищные вещи века!
На душу наложено вето.
Мы в горы уходим и в бороды,
Ныряем голыми в воду,

Но реки мелеют, либо
В морях умирают рыбы...

...Душа моя, мой звереныш,
Меж городских кулис
Щенком с обрывком веревки
Ты носишься и скулишь!

THE BEATNIK'S MONOLOGUE

TO E. NEIZVESTNY

Run—into the self, to Haiti, inside R.C. churches,
                             into privies, Egyptian deserts.
Run!

Machines as dark as Khan Batyi
have enslaved us.

In law courts their barefaced agents,
gulping petrol from wine glasses,
calculate: Who was it in England
led the revolt against machines?
Let us run! . . .

And in the night, overcoming his modesty,
the cybernetic robot makes demands
on his creator:

"Give me your wife!" he says.
"I have a weakness for brunettes," he says.
                             "I love
at thirty revolutions. Better be
                     accommodating! . . ."

O the rapacious things of this age!
The soul is vetoed.
We bolt into the hills, into beards,
dive naked into the water.

But the rivers dry up, for
the fish are dying out in the seas . . .

. . . My soul, my little beast,
behind the city scenes
you scamper about and scowl
like a puppy with a broken leash!

А время свистит красиво
Над огненным Теннессй,
Загадочное, как сирин
С дюралевыми шасси.

ОЗА (IV, V, VI)

IV

А может, милый друг, мы впрямь сентиментальны?
И душу удалят, как вредные миндалины?

Ужели и хорей, серебряный флейтист,
погибнет, как форель погибла у плотин?

Ужели и любовь немодна, как камин?
Аминь?

А почему ж, забыв луга и сосняки,
мы тянемся к стихам, как к травам от цинги?
И радостно и робко в нас души расцветают...
Роботы,
      роботы,
            роботы
речь мою прерывают.

Толпами автоматы
топают к автоматам,
сунут жетон оплаты,
вытянут сок томатный,

And handsomely time whistles
Over fiery Tennessee,
As enigmatic as a siren
With a duralumin chassis.

1962

OZA (Parts IV–V–VI)

I V
Perhaps dear friend, we're downright sentimental?
They'll excise our souls like unwholesome tonsils.

Will the trochee, silver flutist, perish
as trout have died when blocked by river dams?

Is love an old-fashioned fireplace?
Amen to that?

And why, forgetting meadow, pine and grove,
are we drawn to poems as to herbs for curing scurvy?
Then, shyly in us, souls flower in joy . . .
But robots,
            robots,
                    robots,
cut short our speech.

In throngs, automata
tramp towards automata,
drop their coins in,
and tomato juice spills out,

некогда думать, некогда,
в оффисы — как вагонетки,
есть только брутто, нетто —
быть человеком некогда!

Вот мой приятель-лирик:
К нему забежала горничная...
Утром вздохнула горестно —
мол, так и не поговорили!

Ангел, об чем претензии?
Провинциалочка некая!
Сказки хотелось, песни?
Некогда, некогда, некогда!

Что там в груди колотится
пойманной партизанкою?
Сердце, нам безработица.
В мире — роботизация.

Ужас! Мама,
        роди меня обратно!..

Обратно — к истокам неслись реки.

Обратно — от финиша к старту задним ходом неслись мотоциклисты.

Баобабы на глазах, худея, превращались в прутики саженцев — обратно!

Пуля, вылетев из сердца Маяковского, пролетев прожженную дырочку на рубашке, юркнула в ствол маузера 4-03986, а тот, свернувшись улиткой, нырнул в ящик стола...

...Твой отец историк. Он говорит, что человечество имеет обратный возраст. Оно идет от старости к молодости.

Хотя бы средневековье. Старость. Морщинистые стены инквизиции.

no time to think, no time,
in offices, as in coal trams,
there's only gross and net—
no time to be a man!

A maid came running into the room
of a friend of mine, a lyrical poet . . .
Next morning she sighed her frustration—
she hadn't much chance for conversation.

Angel, what are you getting at?
A country girl, that's all she is!
You want me to be lyrical, spout fables?
There's no time, no time, no time!

What is it throbs in the breast
like a partisan girl they've trapped at last?
We're being disemployed, O heart.
The world is turning robot.

How horrible! Mama,
            bear me back—back into the womb! . . .

Back—to their source the rivers rushed.
Back—from finish to start, motorcyclists sped in reverse gear.
Before our eyes, the Baobab trees, shrinking, were being changed into the twigs of newly planted trees—back!
Flying out of Mayakovsky's heart, the bullet darted out of the singed hole in his shirt, dove into the barrel of gun No. 4–03986, and the latter, curling up like a snail, headed for the table-drawer . . .

. . . Your father is an historian. He maintains that mankind is aging in reverse. Passing from old age to youth.
Take the Middle Ages. Old age. The wrinkled walls of the Inquisition.

Потом Ренессанс — бабье лето человечества. Это как женщина, красивая, все познавшая, пирует среди зрелых плодов и тел.

«...Электрон после рассеивания может
двигаться назад во времени. Тогда
обыкновенный позитрон можно рассматривать
как электрон, для которого время течет
вспять (обратное время).

«Теория фундаментальных процессов».

Р. П. Хейнман. Нью-Йорк, 1963.

Не будем перечислять надежд, измен, приключений XVIII века, задумчивой беременности XIX.

А начало XX века — бешеный ритм революции! Восемнадцатилетие командармов. «Мы — первая любовь земли». «Сейчас подымается социализм, живым, человечьим, правдашним». Но было и так...

Голова ли от ветра кружится?
Или память клубком раскручивается?
Будто крутится радиолой
марш охрипший и одиозный.

Ты не пой, пластинка, про Сталина.
Это песенка не простая,
непроста усов седина,
то —- прозрачна, а то — мутна...

Те усы свисали над трубкой
выдьющегося конструктора,
разбирались в шайбочках, в винтиках,
человека только не видели!

Then the Renaissance—the Indian summer of mankind. So like a woman, a beautiful woman who has experienced everything, feasting among ripe fruit and mature bodies.

"*. . . The electron, after scattering,*
can move back in time. Then the
ordinary positron can be regarded
as an electron, for which time flows
backwards (reverse time)".

Theory of Fundamental Processes.

> *R. P. Feynman, New York, 1963.*

Let us not enumerate the hopes, the betrayals, the adventures of the 18th century, the moody pregnancy of the 19th.

Early in the 20th century—the frenzied rhythm of the Revolution! The *Komandarms'* eighteenth birthday. "We are the earth's first love." "Now socialism is on the rise, vital, human, true." But there was also . . .

Is it the wind makes the head turn?
Or memory unwinding like a skein?
It's as though a hoarse and hateful march
were spinning on a phonograph there.

Do not sing, record, about Stalin.
This is no simple little song,
not simple the gray of those mustaches,
which now are clear, now fuzzy gray . . .

Those mustaches drooped over the pipe
of an outstanding engineer;
they made sense of bolts and screws,
but never discerned the human being!

Кто в них верил? И кто в них сгинул,
как иголка в седой копне?
Их разглаживали при Гимне.
Их мочили в красном вине.

И торжественно над страною,
точно птица хищной красы,
плыли
       с красною
              бахромою
государственные усы!
Ты не пой, пластинка, про Сталина.
Быть нам винтиком не пристало.
Было. Больше не угорим
вислым дымом его седин.

«Я думаю о будущем, — продолжает историк, — когда все мечты осуществляются. Техника в добрых руках добра. Бояться техники? Что же, назад в пещеру!..»
Он седой и румяный. Ему улыбаются дети и собаки.

Who believed in them? And who got lost in them,
like a needle in a gray haystack?
They were stroked while the Hymn blared.
They were dipped in red wine.

And majestically above the land,
beautiful as a bird of prey,
they floated,
              those sovereign
                      mustaches,
fringed with red!
Do not sing, record, about Stalin.
We were not fated to become a mere cog.
That had been. No more shall we be asphyxiated
in the drooping smoke of his gray hair.

"I think of the future," the historian continues, "when
all dreams will be realized. In good hands technology is good.
To fear technology? That's to go back to the cave! . . ."
    He's gray and pink. Children and dogs smile at him.

ОТ АВТОРА И КОЕ-ЧТО ДРУГОЕ

Не к первому попала мне тетрадь:
ее командировщики листали,
острили на полях ее устало
и засыпали, силясь разобрать.

Вот чей-то почерк: «Автор-абстрактист!»
А снизу красным: «Сам туда катись!»
«Но машина мыслит...»
«Но она мыслит мыслью чьей? Человека!»

«Может, автор сам из тех, кто
тешит публику подтекстом?»
«Брось искать подтекст: задрыга!
Ты смотришь в книгу —

                 видишь фигу!»

Оставим эти мудрости, дневник.
Хватает комментариев без них.

V
А не махнуть ли мне на море?

VI
В час отлива возле чайной

                я сидел в ночи печальной,
          говорил друзьям об Озе и величье бытия.
но внезапно черный ворон
              примешался к разговорам,
вспыхнув синими очами,
    он сказал:
«А на фига?!»

Я вскричал: «Мне жаль вас, птица,
       человеком вам родиться б,
          счастье высшее трудиться,
             полпланеты раскроя...»
Он сказал: «А на фига?!»

FROM THE AUTHOR AND SOMETHING BESIDES

I was not the first to find this notebook: it,
other men on missions had leafed through
had wearily jotted witty comments in the margin
and had drowsed off, trying to decipher it.

Here's someone's hand: "Author-abstractionist!"
And underneath in red! "Roll there yourself!"
"But the machine can think . . ."
"But whose is the thought behind it? Man's!"

Perhaps the author is one of those
who amuses the public with a subtext?"
"Stop looking for a subtext: you jerk!
You look into a book—
                    a fig's all you find!"

Diary, let's leave these subtleties.
Without them there are enough commentaries.

V
And why shouldn't I take off to the seashore?

VI
At the out-tide hour beside a tearoom
                        I sat in the mournful night,
    talking to friends of Oza and the majesty of being,
but of a sudden a black raven
                    broke into our conversation;
with blue eyes blazing,
                    he declared:
"I don't give a hoot!"

I cried out: "I have pity for you, bird,
                you should have been born a man,
                    the highest happiness is to labor,
                        cutting up half of the planet . . ."
He replied: "I don't give a hoot!"

«Будешь ты, великий ментор,
      бог машин, экспериментов,
            будешь бронзой монументов
                  знаменит во все края...»
Он сказал: «А на фига?!»

«Уничтожив олигархов,
      ты настроишь агрегатов,
            демократией заменишь
                  короля и холуя...»
Он сказал: «А на фига?!»

Я сказал: «А хочешь — будешь
      спать в заброшенной избушке,
            утром пальчики девичьи
                  будут класть на губы вишни,
                        глушь такая, что не слышна
ни хвала и ни хула...»

Он ответил: «Все — мура,
      раб стандарта, царь природы,
            ты свободен без свободы,
                  ты летишь в автомашине,
но машина — без руля...

Оза, Роза ли, стервоза —
                  как скучны метаморфозы,
                        в ящик рано или поздно...
Жизнь была — а на фига?!»

Как сказать ему, подонку,
что живем не чтоб подохнуть, —
чтоб губами тронуть чудо
поцелуя и ручья!

Чудо жить. Необъяснимо.
Кто не жил — что спорить с ними?!

Можно бы — да на фига?

"You will be, great mentor,
    god of machines and experiments,
        you will be the brass of monuments,
            a man of fame in every part . . ."
He replied: "I don't give a hoot!"

"After destroying the oligarchs,
    you'll start building up aggregates,
        with democracy you'll replace
            the monarch and the toady."
He replied: "I don't give a hoot!"

I spoke out: "If you'd rather—you will
    sleep in a lone abandoned cottage;
        a maiden's fingers in the morning
    will drop cherries on your lips;
        in this wilderness you'll hear
            no sound of praise or blame . . ."

He replied: "It's rot, all rot!
    Slave of standard, tsar of nature,
        you are free but have no freedom,
        you go speeding in a car,
            but the car has no driving wheel . . .

Oza, Roza, or Slutoza—
                metamorphoses are a bore,
        sooner or later shove them in a drawer . . .

Life was—not worth a hoot!"

How impress upon him, the low cur,
that we're not living here to croak—
but to touch with our lips the miracle
of a kiss or a running stream!

To live is marvellous. Inexplicable.
Who haven't lived—no use arguing with them!

One might—but why give a hoot?

1964

ЗАМЕРЛИ

Заведи мне ладони за плечи,
обойми,
только губы дыхнут об мои,
только море за спинами плещет.

Наши спины, как лунные раковины,
что замкнулись за нами сейчас.
Мы заслушаемся,
                                          прислонясь.
Мы — как формула жизни двоякая.

На ветру мировых клоунад
заслоняем своими плечами
возникающее меж нами —
как ладонями пламя хранят.

Если правда, душа в каждой клеточке,
свои форточки отвори.
В моих порах
                                стрижами заплещутся
души пойманные твои!

Все становится тайное явным.
Неужели под свистопад,
разомкнувши объятья, завянем —
как раковины не гудят?

А пока нажимай, заваруха,
на скорлупы упругие спин!
Это нас погружает друг в друга.

Спим.

ARRESTED MOTION

Place your palms behind my shoulders,
embrace me,
only your lips breathe on mine,
only the sea splashes behind our backs.

Our backs are like moonlit shells
that instantly close behind us.
We shall listen,
                       leaning on each other.
We're like a twofold formula of life.

In the wind of universal clowning
with our shoulders we screen
what occurs between us—
as one nurses a flame in cupped hands.

If it's true we have a soul in each cell,
then open your smallest windows.
In my pores
                your captive souls
will start dancing like sandpipers.

All that is hidden comes to light.
Can it be that, breaking from our embrace,
we shall wither in the autumn blast—
like seashells that have ceased to sound?

In the meantime press, you broil of trouble,
on the resilient shells of our backs!
This plunges us deeper into each other.

We sleep.

1965

ЛЕНЬ

Благословенна лень, томительнейший плен,
когда проснуться лень и сну отдаться лень.

Лень к телефону встать, и ты через меня
дотянешься к нему, переутомлена.

Рождающийся звук в тебе, как колокольчик,
и диафрагмою мое плечо щекочет.

«Билеты? — скажешь ты. — Пусть пропадают. Лень».
Медлительнейший день в нас переходит в тень.

Лень — двигатель прогресса. Ключ к Диогену — лень.
Я знаю: ты прелестна,
                                все остальное — тлен.

Вселенная дурит? До завтрего потерпит.
Лень телеграмму взять — заткните под портьеру.

Лень ужинать идти, лень выключить «трень-брень».
И лень окончить мысль:
                                сегодня воскресень...

Июнь среди дороги
Разлегся подшофе
Сатиром козлоногим,
Босой и в галифе.

LAZINESS

Blessed be laziness, langorous captivity,
when we're too lazy even to wake, too lazy to sleep.

Too lazy to answer the telephone, and you,
languid you, will have to reach across me.

The sound born in you tinkles like a bell,
and tickles my shoulder with the receiver.

"Tickets?" you'll ask. "Can't be bothered. Too lazy."
In us the long delaying day passes into shade.

Laziness, lever of progress. Laziness, key to Diogenes.
I know you're lovely,
                            all else is mere dross.

Is the universe fooling? It will hold out till tomorrow.
Too lazy to receive a telegram—shove it under the curtain.

Too lazy to go to supper, too lazy to switch off the "jingle-jangle,"
And too lazy to complete a thought:
                            today is Sund . . . .

June in the middle of the road
has stretched out a trifle looped
a goat-footed satyr
barefoot and in riding breeches.

1965

ШЕСТЬ СТРОФ С ИРОНИЕЙ

В дни неслыханно болевые
быть без сердца — мечта.
Чемпионы лупили навылет —
ни черта!

Продырявленный, точно решета,
утешаю ажиотаж:
«Поглазейте в меня, как в решетку, —
так шикарен пейзаж!»

Но неужто узнает ружье,
где,
          привязана нитью болезненной,
бьешься ты в миллиметре от лезвия,
ахиллесово
                    сердце
                              мое?!

Тсс, любимая, тише...
Нашумело меняя места,
я ношусь по России —
                              как птица
отвлекает огонь от гнезда.

Все болишь? Ночами пошаливаешь?
Беззащитно спасителен плюс.
Не касайтесь рукою шершавою —
от судороги валюсь.

Невозможно расправиться с нами.
Невозможнее — выносить.
Но еще невозможней —
                              что снайпер
перережет дрожащую нить!

SIX STROPHES WITH IRONY

In unheard of days of sickness,
it's a dream to have no heart.
Champions punched right through—
to no effect!

Full of holes like a sieve,
I comfort the agiotage:
"Look at me as through a grating—
that way the landscape is more *chic*!"

But will a rifle pick out
where,
            tied to a sickly thread,
you throb a millimeter from the blade,
my
        Achilles
                heart!?

Shush . . . , my beloved, be quiet . . .
All that noise of moving from place to place.
I scurry through Russia—
                            like a bird
that draws fire away from the nest.

You're still sick! Play pranks at night!
The advantage was defenselessly saving!
Do not touch me with your rough hand—
I collapse in convulsions.

It's impossible to make short shrift of us.
More impossible to bear it.
And more impossible still—
                            for a sniper
to snap the quivering thread.

1965

NOVELLA MATVEYEVA

1935-

Few facts are available as yet about this young woman poet who began to emerge in the early 1960's. She was brought up in a children's home, and has spent much time in hospitals. Her lyrical poems, all of a certain length, have a distinctly personal note. Her reputation is steadily growing. As the volume of her work increases, she is likely to become a poet of importance. Her recent long poem, "Hypnosis" (1965), would seem to confirm the developing quality of her imagination and sensitivity to language. She often manages to create a dreamlike atmosphere in a country or city scene—an atmosphere rare in Soviet poetry. Matveyeva has published in almanacs and magazines, and also three volumes of verse, of which the latest is *The Soul of Things* (1966). Matveyeva lives mostly in Moscow and Peredelkino.

Я, говорит, не воин,
Я, говорит, раздвоен,
Я, говорит, расстроен,
Расчетверен,
Распят!
Ты, говорю, не воин,
Ты, говорю, раздвоен,
Распят и четвертован,
Но ты не из растяп.
Покуривая трубку,
Себя, как мясорубку,
На части разобрав,
Ты, может быть, и прав.
Но знаешь? Этой ночью
К тебе придут враги;
Я вижу их воочью,
Я слышу их шаги...
Ты слышишь?
Не слышишь?
Они уже спешат...
Они идут, как мыши,
На твой душевный склад.
И вскорости растащат
Во мраке и в тиши
Отколотые части
Твоей больной души.
— А что же будут делать
Они с моей душой?
А что же будут делать

I, HE SAYS, AM NO WARRIOR

I, he says, am no warrior,
I, he says, am split in two,
I, he says, am disturbed,
Quartered,
Crucified!
You, I say, are no warrior,
You, I say, are split in two,
Crucified and quartered,
But you are no bungler.
Puffing at a pipe,
Taking yourself apart
As one does a meat-grinder,
You may well be right.
But you had better know! This night
Enemies will come to you;
I see them very plainly,
I hear their footsteps approaching . . .
You hear them!
You don't hear them?
They're already hurrying . . .
Like mice, they're scampering
Towards your spiritual larder.
And briskly they will steal
In darkness and in quiet
The splintered portions
Of your ailing spirit.
"And what will they start doing
To this soul of mine?"
And what will they start doing

С разбитой, но большой?
— Вторую часть покрасят,
А третью — разлинуют,
Четвертую заквасят,
А пятую раздуют,
Шестую подожгут,
А сами убегут.
Был человек не воин,
Был человек раздвоен,
Был человек разрознен,
А все, должно быть, врал:
Прослышав о напасти,
Мигать он начал чаще,
И сгреб он эти части,
И — ничего! — собрал.

To that soul all smashed, but ample?"
"They'll paint the second part,
And they will rule the third;
The fourth they will ferment,
And they'll inflate the fifth,
The sixth they'll set on fire,
And then take to their heels.
There was a man, no warrior,
There was a man who's split in two,
There was a man that's incomplete,
And all the time he must have lied:
Then hearing of disaster,
He began to wink more often,
And raked these parts together,
And—passably!—gathered them into one.

1965

Вам хочется чудес?
Религий? Но откуда
Вы взяли, что не чудо —
Хотя бы этот лес?
Хотя бы этот брег
С корявыми камнями,
Хотя бы этот снег
С бегущими тенями,
Хотя бы — человек,
А именно — вы сами?

Вам кажется кощунством,
Что ваш волшебный сон,
Волшебным полный чувством,
Научно объяснен?

Откуда ж ваша мука
И ваша боль — откуда?
На свете есть наука,
И это тоже — чудо
Ничем не хуже сна.
И даже неизвестно,
Что более чудесно:
Ваш сон или она...

Колодец наш бездонный
Пополнен — чуть иссяк:
Мечте — и объясненной —
Остаться в чудесах.

И после пояснений,
Кто и откуда он, —
Все той же тайной гений
Пребудет окружен.

YOU WISH FOR MIRACLES

You wish for miracles!
Religions! But who told
You it's no miracle—
This forest, at least!
This shore, at the very least,
With its knobbly rocks;
This snow, at the very least,
With its running shadows,
This man, at the very least,
The man who is yourself.

It seems to you a sacrilege,
That your so marvelous dream,
So full of marvelous feeling,
Should be explained by science!

Whence comes your torment
And your pain—tell me wherefrom?
There's science in this world,
And this is no less
A miracle than dreaming.
And it is even still unknown
Which is the greater miracle:
our science or your dream . . .

Our bottomless well is full—
hardly drained at all:
Our illusion—even if explained—
Will remain one of a miracle.

Even after explication—
Who he is and whence—
The genius will remain
By the same mystery surrounded.

1965

ВОДОСТОЧНЫЕ ТРУБЫ

Дождь,
Дождь вечерний
Сквозь водосточные трубы...
Мокрые стены,
Зеленая плесень да мох...
Ах, эти трубы!
Сделали трубочкой губы,
Чтобы прохожим
Выболтать тайны домов.

Трубы вы, трубы!
Я вашим тайнам не рада.
Ржавые трубы,
Вы бросьте про тайны трубить!
Я вас не знаю,
Мне ваших секретов не надо:
Зная секреты,
Трудно мечтать и любить.

Верю, ах, верю
Тому, что за этою дверью
И в том окошке —
Обида, утрата, обман...
Верю, ах, верю!
Но почему-то не верю
И улыбаюсь
Каменным этим домам.

THE GUTTERS

Rain,
Evening rain
Gushing through gutters . . .
Damp walls,
Green mildew and lichen . . .
Ah, these gutters!
They have furled their lips into pipes,
To spill out to the passersby
The secrets of the houses.

Gutters, you gutters!
I'm not glad of your secrets.
Rusty gutters,
Stop trumpeting about secrets!
I don't know you.
I have no need of your secrets:
Knowing secrets,
It is hard to dream and to love.

I believe, ah! I believe
In what is behind that door
And at the window—
Hurt, loss, deceit . . .
I believe, ah! I believe.
But for some reason I do not believe
And I smile
At these houses of stone.

Верю надежде —
Даже как будто напрасной;
Даже напрасной,
Совсем невозможной мечте;
Вижу я город,
Вижу я город прекрасный —
В белом тумане,
В черном вечернем дожде...

Трубы вы, трубы!
Бедные, вы еще стары!
Вся ваша плесень —
Лишь первый пушок над губой...
Вы еще стары,
А мы уже юными стали,
Хоть мы узнали
Самую старую боль.

Дождь...
Дождь вечерний
Сквозь водосточные трубы...
Мокрые стены,
Зеленая плесень да мох...
Ах, эти трубы!
Сделали трубочкой губы,
Чтобы
Прохожим
Выболтать тайны домов.

I believe in hope—
Even in hope that seems vain;
Even in hope that is vain,
In a quite impossible dream;
I see a city,
I see a beautiful city—
Wrapped in white mist,
In black evening rain . . .

Gutters, you gutters!
Poor gutters, you are still old!
All of your mildew
Resembles the first down above a lip . . .
You are still old,
While we have already grown young,
Though we have learned
The oldest of pains.

Rain . . .
Evening rain
Gushing through gutters . . .
Damp walls,
The green mildew and lichen . . .
Ah! these gutters!
They have furled their lips into pipes
In order to spill out
To the passersby
The secrets of the houses.

1965

LEONID GUBANOV

1947–

A precocious and rebellious Moscow schoolboy of working class background who has recently emerged as a poet with a protesting voice, Gubanov has been published mainly in the "underground" little reviews produced by *SMOG*. One poem of his has, however, appeared in the established magazine *Yunost*. In the summer of 1965 four of his poems were included in *Sphinxes*, an unofficial poetry magazine edited by Valery Tarsis. Gubanov is also a painter, and his poem "The Artist" reflects not only his preoccupation with art, but also his rebellious spirit in the tradition of Gauguin.

ХУДОЖНИК

Холст 37 на 37.
Такого же размера рамка.
Мы умираем не от рака
И не от старости совсем.

Когда изжогой мучит дело,
Нас тянут краски теплой плотью.
Уходим в ночь от жен и денег.
На полнолуние полотен.

Да, мазать мир! Да, кровью вен!
Забыв болезни, сны, обеты!
И умирать из века в век
На голубых руках мольберта.

THE ARTIST

The canvas is 37 by 37.
The frame is of a size to fit.
We are not dying because of cancer,
And not altogether of old age.

When we suffer heartburn in our quest,
The warm flesh of colors pulls us after.
We go into the night, leaving wives and money,
To find a harvest moon of canvases.

Yes, paint the world! Yes, with our veins' blood!
Forgetting our sickness, our dreams and vows!
And let us die from age to age
In the azure arms of an easel.

1964

IVAN KHARABAROV

1940 (?)–

Five of Ivan Kharabarov's poems, including "I'm All Of Rough Bark" and "Christmas Tree," were first printed in *Syntaksis I* (Moscow, December 1959). Since then Kharabarov's poems have appeared in some of the established magazines and almanacs. The two poems here printed have a certain vigor and expressiveness, though not the note of foreboding and disquiet to be found in some other of his earlier poems. So far few facts are available about his origins and life, but he seems quite familiar with the Siberian landscape.

Я весь из шершавой коры.
Я весь
　　　из сосновой хвои.
Я пришел
　　　　эту землю укрыть,
уберечь от болезни и хвори.
Я пришел из тайги,
тяжелы и темны мои руки,
мои корни — туги,
мои ветки — упруги.
А в нездешних очах —
слезы
　　　жгучи и солоны,
на смолистых плечах
дремлют
　　　　черные соболи.
Принесу я весну
лесам этим
　　　　　чахлым и редким,
я прохладу верну
этим
　　　теплым и мутным рекам.
Я плохого не сделаю,
вам не быть
　　　　　на меня в обиде.
Я всего лишь
　　　　зеленое дерево,
не рубите меня —
　　　　　　любите.

I'M ALL OF ROUGH BARK

I'm all of rough bark.
I'm all
           of pine branch.
I have come
               to spread over this land,
to preserve it from sickness and ailment.
I have come from the taiga,
my hands are heavy and dark,
my roots are tough,
my branches resilient.
And to a stranger's eyes,
my tears
            are scalding and salt;
on my pine resin shoulders
black sables
              drowse.
I shall bring springtime
to these sparse
                and stunted forests;
I shall bring back coolness
to these
          warm, turbid rivers.
I shall do no harm,
you'll have no cause to complain
                          against me.
I am merely
            a green tree;
Do not cut me down—
                  love me instead.

1959

ЕЛКА

Лишь качание
                    маятника,
да шорох
              за дверью...
Почему
        я не маленький
и в сказки
            не верю?
Здравствуй, елочка,
                        елка,
золотая иголка,
смуглые лапы,
светлые лампы.
Ты зеленая,
              красная,
темная
        синяя —
такая разная
и красивая.
Ты приходишь не часто.
Ты приходишь, чтоб люди
не забыли о счастье,
не разверились в чуде.
Ты немного смешная
и чуточку грустная —
такая большая
и такая
          игрушечная!

CHRISTMAS TREE

Just a pendulum
                    swinging,
and a rustling sound
                        behind the door . . .
Why am I
            not a child,
and why don't I believe
                        in fairy tales?
Good day, little tree,
                    Christmas tree,
golden needle,
smooth paws,
bright lights.
You are green,
                scarlet,
dark
      and deep blue—
so varied
and beautiful.
You do not come very often.
You arrive to remind people
not to forget about happiness,
not to disbelieve in miracle.
You have your funny side
and you are a trifle sad—
you so large
and so
        like a toy!

1959

YURY GALANSKOV

1940–

Yury Galanskov is a poet whom we first encounter, represented by two long poems, in *Phoenix* I (Moscow, 1961)—the "underground" mimeographed magazine that circulated clandestinely in Moscow following the enforced disbandenment of its predecessor *Syntaksis* Nos. I, II and III. Galanskov's poem, "The Human Manifesto," written apparently with deliberation in the aggressive style of Mayakovsky's earlier poetry (*The Cloud In Trousers*, for example), is remarkable for its spirit of revolt and violent tone, which differed from anything to be found in the milder, more "lonely" spirit of *Syntaksis*.

A former student of Moscow University (expelled because of his contribution to *Phoenix* I), Galanskov claims to be a democrat and pacifist. He has taken part in protest demonstrations in front of the Mayakovsky Monument and the U.S. Embassy in Moscow (See "The Washington Post" of June 12, 1965). He was also editor of *Phoenix 1966* (December), which was full of provocative "underground" material and also included his "Open Letter to M. Sholokhov," defending Sinyavsky and Daniel. As a result, he was arrested in the third week of January, 1967, together with three other contributors. These arrests led to a protest meeting at the Pushkin Monument on January 22.

ЧЕЛОВЕЧЕСКИЙ МАНИФЕСТ

1

Всё чаще и чаще в ночной тиши
вдруг начинаю рыдать.
Ведь даже крупицу богатств души
уже невозможно отдать.
Никому не нужно:
в поисках Идиота
так измотаешься за день!
А люди идут, отработав,
туда, где деньги и бляди.
И пусть.
Сквозь людскую лавину
я пройду, непохожий, один —
как будто кусок рубина,
сверкающий между льдин.
Небо!
Хочу сиять я.
Ночью мне разреши
на бархате черного платья
рассыпать алмазы души.

2

Министрам, вождям и газетам — не верьте!
Вставайте, лежащие ниц!
Видите — шарики атомной смерти
у мира в могилах глазниц.
Вставайте!
Вставайте!
Вставайте!
О, алая кровь бунтарства!
Идите и доломайте
гнилую тюрьму государства!
Идите по трупам пугливых
тащить для голодных людей
черные бомбы, как сливы,
на блюдища площадей.

THE HUMAN MANIFESTO

1

Ever more often in the quiet of the night
I suddenly burst into sobs.
For it's already impossible
to give away even a granule of spiritual riches.
Nobody needs it:
in quest of the Idiot,
what wear and tear during the day!
And people, having finished their day's work,
go where they find money and whores.
And let them.
Through the avalanche of people
I shall pass, unlike them, alone—
glittering like a lump of ruby
among icebergs.
Sky!
I wish to shine.
Allow me in the night
to sprinkle the diamonds of my soul
on the velvet of a black dress.

2

Ministers, leaders and newspapers—do not believe them!
Arise, you who are lying face down!
You see the little balls of atomic death
the world has in the graves of its sockets.
Rise!
Rise!
Rise!
O, the scarlet blood of rebellion!
Go forth and finish breaking up
the rotten prison of the state!
March over the corpses of the timid
to haul for the benefit of the famished
black bombs, like plums,
on the plates of the public squares.

3
Где они —
те, кто нужны,
чтобы горло пушек зажать;
чтобы вырезать язвы войны
священным ножом мятежа.
Где они?
Где они?
Где они?
Или их вовсе нет? —
Вон — у станков их тени
прикованы горстью монет.

4
Человек исчез.
Ничтожный, как муха,
он еле шевелится в строчках книг.
Выйду на площадь
и городу в ухо
втисну отчаянья крик...
А потом, пистолет достав,
прижму его крепко к виску...
Не дам никому растоптать
души белоснежный лоскут.
Люди!
Оставьте, не надо...
Бросьте меня утешать.
Всё равно среди вашего ада
мне уже нечем дышать!
Приветствуйте Подлость и Голод!
А я, поваленный наземь,
плюю в ваш железный город,
набитый деньгами и грязью.

3

Where are they—
those needed
to throttle the guns;
to excise the sores of war
with the sacred knife of insurrection?
Where are they?
Where are they?
Where are they?
Or are they nowhere at all?
There—a handful of coins chains
Their shadows to the benches.

4

Man has disappeared.
Insignificant as a fly
he hardly stirs among the lines in books.
I shall go out into the public square
and into the city's ear
I'll thrust my shout of despair . . .
And then, getting hold of a gun,
I shall press it firmly against my temple . . .
I shall not allow anybody to trample on
a shred of the snow-white soul.
People!
Leave me alone, I don't need it . . .
Stop trying to console me.
In the midst of your hell
I have nothing to breathe anyway!
Welcome baseness and famine!
And I, thrown to the ground,
spit on your city of iron,
stuffed full of money and filth.

5

Небо!
Не знаю, что делаю...
Мне бы карающий нож!
Видишь, как кто-то на белое
выплеснул черную ложь.
Видишь,
как вечера тьма
жует окровавленный стяг...
И жизнь страшна, как тюрьма,
воздвигнутая на костях.
Падаю!
Падаю!
Падаю!
Вам оставляю лысеть.
Не стану питаться падалью —
как все.
Не стану кишкам на потребу
плоды на могилах срезать.
Не нужно мне вашего хлеба,
замешанного на слезах.
И падаю, и взлетаю
в полубреду,
в полусне...
И чувствую, как расцветает
человеческое
во мне.

5
Sky!
I don't know what I'm doing . . .
O that I had a chastising knife.
You see how somebody has splashed
black lies upon white.
You see
The dark of the evening
chewing a blood-bespattered flag . . .
And life is as terrible as a prison,
erected upon a pile of bones.
I fall!
I fall!
I fall!
I leave you to grow bald.
I shall not feed on offal
as all do.
For the use of my guts I shall not
cut down fruit on graves.
I have no need of your bread,
kneaded from tears.
I fall and soar
in semi-delirium,
in semi-sleep . . .
I feel humanity
flowering
in me.

6

Привыкли видеть,
расхаживая
вдоль улиц в свободный час,
лица, жизнью изгаженные,
такие же, как у вас.
И вдруг —
словно грома раскаты
и словно явление миру Христа —
восстала
растоптанная и распятая
человеческая красота.
Это — я,
призывающий к правде и бунту,
не желающий больше служить,
рву ваши черные путы,
сотканные из лжи.
Это — я,
законом закованный,
кричу человеческий манифест!
И пусть мне ворон выклевывает
на мраморе тела
крест!

6

You're accustomed to see,
as you stroll
along the streets in a leisure hour,
faces as distorted
as your own.
And suddenly—
like thunder pealing,
like Christ manifesting Himself to the world—
there ascended
a trampled and crucified
human beauty.
It is—I,
summoning you to truth and revolt,
desiring to serve no longer,
who tear your black fetters,
all woven of falsehood.
It is—I,
bound by the bonds of the law,
who shout forth the human manifesto!
And may a raven peck out
a cross
on the marble of my body.

1961

IOSIF BRODSKY

1940–

Iosif Brodsky presents a rather special case since 1964. In February-March of that year he was tried in Leningrad and sentenced to five years hard labor in the Archangel region on the grounds that he was a *tuneyadetz* or "parasite." The indications are that the charges against him were trumped up and that the trial itself was unfair. In any case, it was reported only in two Leningrad newspapers. In the West, however, Brodsky's trial was more widely reported. It is known that several well known Soviet writers and intellectuals pleaded on Brodsky's behalf—to no avail. A number of Soviet writers have a high regard for Brodsky's work as a poet and the late Anna Akhmatova, in particular, thought of him as the outstanding poet of the younger generation. But Brodsky has to date no official status as a poet. A body of his poems has been received and printed in Russian in the U.S.A. But otherwise, in the Soviet Union, only five poems of his are known to have been published. Most of the Brodsky poems we know were written by him before the age of twenty-three. It is too early to judge, except to say that he shows definite talent and originality, and a wide grasp of forms and rhythms. In many poems his attitude is that of isolation and even, perhaps, melancholy. He has written many night-pieces, and in the *Big Elegy* (about John Donne) he has shown himself capable of writing a sustained longer poem, though an essentially lyrical one.

In the light of his work and mishaps, it is interesting to note a few meager facts about his biography. He was born in Leningrad of a Jewish family and left school at fifteen. Apparently he worked for a year as a cutter and took part in geological expeditions. He has also succeeded in mastering several languages, among them English and Spanish. He was a member of the translators' section of the Leningrad Union of Writers. At his trial, he defined his profession as that of "poet-translator."

РЫБЫ ЗИМОЙ

Рыбы зимой живут.
Рыбы жуют кислород.
Рыбы зимой плывут,
задевая глазами лед.
Туда.
      Где глубже.
Где море.
Рыбы.
    Рыбы.
        Рыбы.
Рыбы плывут зимою.
Рыбы хотят выплыть.
Рыбы плывут без света.
Под солнцем
       зимним и зыбким.
Рыбы плывут от смерти
вечным путем
      рыбьим.
      Рыбы не льют слезы;
    упираясь головой
          в глыбы,
  в холодной воде
  мерзнут
  холодные глаза
  рыбы.
Рыбы
    всегда молчаливы,
ибо они —
      безмолвны.
Стихи о рыбах,
        как рыбы,
встают поперек
горла.

FISH IN WINTER

Fish live in winter.
Fish chew oxygen.
Fish swim in winter,
catching the ice with their eyes.
Yonder.
       Where it's deeper.
Out to sea.
Fish.
    Fish.
       Fish.
Fish swim in winter.
Fish want to surface.
Fish swim without light.
Beneath a wintry,
             wavering sun.
Fish swim from death,
following their eternal
      fish route.
      Fish don't shed tears;
      they press their heads against
            blocks of ice;
      and their cold eyes
      of fish
      freeze
      in the chill water.
      Fish
          are ever taciturn,
      for they
             are mute.
      Poems about fish,
               like fish,
    stick
    in your throat.

1960–62

ПАМЯТНИК ПУШКИНУ

«...И Пушкин падает в голубоватый колючий снег...»

Эдуард Багрицкий.

...И тишина.
И более ни слова.
И эхо.
Да еще усталость.
...Свои стихи
доканчивая кровью,
они на землю
глухо опускались.
Потом глядели медленно
и нежно.
Им было дико, холодно
и странно.
Над ними наклонялись безнадежно
седые доктора и секунданты.
Над ними звезды, вздрагивая,
пели,
над ними останавливались
ветры...
          ...Пустой бульвар.
И пение метели.
Пустой бульвар.
И памятник поэту.

Пустой бульвар.
И пение метели.
И голова
опущена устало.

...В такую ночь
ворочаться в постели
приятней,
          чем стоять
на пьедесталах.

THE MONUMENT TO PUSHKIN

"And Pushkin falls into the bluish prickly snow . . ."

Eduard Bagritzky

. . . And silence.
And no word more.
And echo.
And weariness too.
Ending their poems
with blood,
they dully dropped
                    to earth.
Slowly then they stared,
and tenderly.
They felt wild and chill
and strange.
Hopelessly above them
the seconds and the gray doctors stooped.
Stars sang above them,
shuddering;
the winds paused
above them . . .
                    A deserted boulevard.
And the blizzard singing.
A deserted boulevard.
And the poet's monument.

A deserted boulevard.
And the blizzard singing.
And a head
wearily drooping.

. . . On such a night
to turn and toss in bed
is far more pleasant
                    than to be standing
on a pedestal.

1960–62

...Был черный небосвод светлей тех ног,
и слиться с темнотою он не мог.
В тот вечер возле нашего огня
Увидели мы черного коня.

Не помню я чернее ничего.
Как уголь были ноги у него.
Он черен был, как ночь, как пустота.
Он черен был от гривы до хвоста.
Но черной по другому уж была
спина его, не знавшая седла.
Недвижно он стоял; казалось, спит.
Пугала чернота его копыт.

Он черен был, не чувствовал теней.
Так черен, что не делался темней.
Так черен, как полуночная мгла.
Так черен, как внутри себя игла.
Так черен, как деревья впереди.
Как место между ребрами в груди.
Как ямка под землею, где зерно.
Я думаю: внутри у нас черно.

Но все-таки чернел он на глазах!
Была всего лишь полночь на часах.
Он к нам не приближался ни на шаг.
В паху его царил бездонный мрак.
Спина его была уж не видна.
Не оставалось светлого пятна.
Глаза его белели, как щелчок.
Еще страшнее был его зрачок.

THE SKY'S BLACK VAULT

The sky's black vault was brighter than those legs,
And with the darkness it could not blend.
That evening, close to our bonfire,
We caught sight of the black horse.

I can remember nothing blacker—
His legs were black as coal.
He was as black as night, as the void,
He was black from mane to tail.
But his back, unaccustomed to the saddle,
Was blacker in another way.
He stood quite motionless; seemed to sleep.
The blackness of his hooves inspired fear.

He was black, impervious to shadows.
So black, he could have grown no blacker.
As black he was as darkest midnight.
As black as the inside of a needle.
As black as the trees before us.
As that place in the chest between the ribs.
As a hole in the ground, where lies a seed.
I think it must be black inside us.

Yet he kept growing blacker to our eyes!
It was only midnight by the clock.
He moved no nearer to us, not a step.
In his groin abysmal darkness reigned.
His back was visible no longer.
No patch of light remained there.
His eyes gleamed white, like a flicked fingernail.
His pupil was even more terrifying.

Как будто он был чей-то негатив!
Зачем же он, свой бег остановив
меж нами оставался до утра?
Зачем не отходил он от костра?
Зачем он черным воздухом дышал,
раздавленными сучьями шуршал?
Зачем струил он черный свет из глаз?

Он всадника искал себе средь нас.

Я обнял эти плечи и взглянул
На то, что оказалось за спиною,
И увидал, что выдвинутый стул
Сливался с освещенною стеною.
Был в лампочке повышенный накал,
Невыгодный для мебели истертой,
И потому диван в углу сверкал
Коричневою кожей, словно желтой.
Стол пустовал, поблескивал паркет,
Темнела печка, в рамке запыленной
Застыл пейзаж, и лишь один буфет.
Казался мне тогда одушевленным.
Но мотылек по комнате кружил,
И он мой взгляд с недвижимости сдвинул,
И если призрак здесь когда то жил,
То он покинул этот дом, покинул.

He was like some person's negative!
Why then, arresting his course,
did he delay with us till morning?
Why did he not leave our bonfire?
Why, stirring the trampled leaves,
did he breathe that black air?
Why did his eyes pour out black light?

He was seeking a rider in our midst!

1960–62

I THREW MY ARMS

I threw my arms about those shoulders, glancing
at what emerged behind that back,
and saw a chair pushed slightly forward,
merging now with the lighted wall.
The lamp glared too bright to show
the shabby furniture to some advantage,
and that is why the sofa of brown leather
shone a sort of yellow in a corner.
The table looked bare, the parquet glossy,
the stove quite dark, and in a dusty frame
a landscape did not stir. Only the sideboard
seemed to me to have some animation.
But a moth flitted round the room,
causing my arrested glance to shift;
and if at any time a ghost had lived here,
he now was gone, abandoning this house.

February 2, 1962

Садовник в ватнике, как дрозд,
по лестнице на ветку влез,
тем самым перекинув мост
к пернатым от двуногих здесь.

Но, вместо щебетанья, вдруг,
в лопатках возбуждая дрожь,
раздался характерный звук:
звук трения ножа о нож.

Вот в этом-то у певчих птиц
с двуногими и весь разрыв
(не меньший, чем в строеньи лиц),
что ножницы, как клюв раскрыв,

на дереве в разгар зимы,
скрипим, а не поем как раз,
Не слишком ли отстали мы
от тех, кто «отстает от нас»?

Помножив краткость бытия
на гнездышки и забытье
при пеньи, полагаю я,
мы место уточним свое.

THRUSHLIKE, THE GARDENER

Thrushlike, the gardener in a quilted coat
Clambered up a ladder on to a branch,
bridging thereby the gap between
the feathered folk and the two-legged here.

But suddenly, instead of a twittering,
a characteristic sound broke out,
sending a shudder down the spine:
the grinding sound of knife on knife.

The great gap between the two-legged species
and the songsters (a gap no less than a face
of different structure) consists in this,
that, with shears gaping like a beak,

we keep on grinding, but do not sing,
when we're up a tree in the thick of winter.
Have we not fallen then too far behind
those who are said "to lag behind us"?

Multiplying in our brief existence
little nests and moments of
forgetfulness in song, I assume,
we shall as yet define our place.

January 18, 1964

Все чуждо в доме новому жильцу.
Поспешный взгляд скользит по всем предметам,
чьи тени так пришельцу не к лицу,
что сами слишком мучаются этим.
Но дом не хочет больше пустовать.
И, как бы за нехваткой той отваги,
замок, не в состояньи узнавать,
один сопротивляется во мраке.
Да, сходства нет меж нынешним и тем,
кто внес сюда шкафы и стол и думал,
что больше не покинет этих стен,
но должен был уйти; ушел и умер.
Ничем уж их нельзя соединить:
чертой лица, характером, надломом.
Но между ними существует нить,
обычно именуемая домом.

ALL THINGS IN THE HOUSE

All things in the house seem strange to the new lodger.
A hurried glance slides over all the objects,
whose shadows are so alien to the newcomer
that even they are too much perturbed.
But the house will not stay vacant any longer.
And as though for lack of that undaunted courage,
the lock, in no state to inquire further,
resists in darkness all alone.
No, who's here bears no resemblance to the person
that had installed the cupboards and the table, thinking
he would leave these walls no more,
but was obliged to leave; had left and died.
There's nothing can bring these two together:
no facial line, no blemish, no trait of character.
Nevertheless, there is a thread that joins,
a thread we usually call a house.

1964

Колесник умер, бондарь
уехал в Архангельск к жене,
и как бык, бушует январь
им вослед на гумне.
А спаситель бадей
стоит меж чужих людей
и слышит вокруг
только шуршание брюк.

Тут от взглядов косых
горяча, как укол —
сбивается русский язык,
бормоча в протокол.
А бесвестный Гефест
глядит, как прошил окрест
снежную гладь канвой
вологодский конвой.

По выходе из тюрьмы,
он в деревне лесной,
в арьергарде зимы,
чинит бочки весной
и в овале бадьи
видит лицо судьи
Савельевой и тайком
в лоб стучит молотком.

THE WHEELWRIGHT DIED

The wheelwright died, the cooper
went off to his wife in Archangel,
and in their wake on the barn floor
January rages like a bull.
And now the saviour of tubs
stands alone among strangers,
and all he hears around him
is the rustling of trousers.

Here, from the scowling looks
that scar like a needle,
the Russian language stumbles
into a mumbled protocol.
And the anonymous Hephaestus
observes the convoy, Vologda-bound,
stitching the flat snow plain
with canvas all around.

On being released from prison,
now that winter's in the rearguard,
he mends in some woodland village
barrels in the spring season,
and in the oval of a tub
beholds the face of Judge
Savelieva, and with his hammer
furtively taps on her forehead.

1964

Original Russian Sources and Bibliography

The sources of the poems and the bibliographical data relevant to the individual poets included in this volume are here presented under the following headings:

> A = original Russian sources
> B = published books
> C = almanacs, magazines, and newspapers

The material under B and C is not necessarily exhaustive. In certain cases, it has proved more difficult to obtain factual data. It should also be noted that, as a rule, the year 1953 serves as a general point of departure for the bibliography.

A number of abbreviations are used, as follows: A.R.S.P. = *Antologia Russkoy Sovietskoy Poezii* (*Anthology of Russian Soviet Poetry*); M = Moscow; L = Leningrad; S.P. = *Sovietski Pisatel* i.e., Soviet Writer (Publishing House); M.G. = *Molodaya Gvardia* i.e., Young Guard (Publishing House), as distinct from the literary magazine of that name; *Gosizdat* = The State Publishing House; *Goslitizdat* = The State Literary Publishing House; *izd. Khud. Lit.* = Publishing House of Artistic Literature.

Soviet poets, who are members of the Union of Soviet Writers, usually publish in the established magazines, such as *Novy Mir* (*The New World*), *Znamya* (*Banner*), *Yunost* (*Youth*), *Zvezda* (*Star*), and so on. There are also the annual Almanacs, such as *Den Poezii* (*Day of Poetry*), published in Moscow, Leningrad, Tbilisi, and other towns. Poems are occasionally printed in the political dailies. A new, less official phenomenon has been the circulation since 1959 of a number of mimeographed Almanacs, such as *Syntaksis*, *Phoenix*, and *Sphinxes*, which usually present the work of younger, less known poets.

BORIS PASTERNAK

A

The poems are from *Phoenix* I and *Novy Mir*, No. 1, 1965.

B

I. Soviet Editions of Pasternak's Poems Since 1953

A.R.S.P. (*Anthology*), vol. 1. Gosizdat. M. 1957. Twelve poems —1925-44.

Stikhotvoreniya i Poemi (Poetical Works and Long Poems). Gosizdat. M. 1957. [This volume, though set up, was never published as a result of the *Doctor Zhivago* incident.]

Stikhotvoreniya i Poemi. Gosizdat. M. 1961. Pp. 376. This is the first Soviet posthumous edition of a selection of Pasternak's poems. It omits the *Zhivago* poems, some of which were included in the abortive 1957 edition, but contains 35 of the *Kogda Razgulyaetsya (A Rift in the Clouds)* cycle, 1956–60.

Stikhotvoreniya i Poemi. Introduction by A. D. Sinyavsky. Compiled with Notes by L. A. Ozerov. S.P. M. 1965. Pp. 732. This edition includes 16 of the *Zhivago* poems and 37 of the *Razgulyaetsya* cycle.

Stikhi. Selected by Z. and E. Pasternak. Intro. by Kornei Chukovsky. Essay "The Poet's Path" by N. Bannikov. izd. Khud. Lit. M. 1966. Pp. 368.

II. *Some Russian Editions Published Outside the Soviet Union*

Poezia. Izbrannoye (Poetry. Selected). Posev. Frankfurt/Main. 1960. Pages 424. Includes the 25 *Zhivago* poems and 42 of the *Razgulyaetsya* ones.

Sochineniya (Works), in 4 vols. Ann Arbor. The University of Michigan Press. 1961. [Vol. 1, *Stikhi i Poemi 1912–1932*; vol. 2, *Prosa 1915–1958*; vol. 3, *Stikhi 1936–1959. Stikhi 1912–1957* (i.e., verse not included in any previous edition). *Stati i Vistupleniya (Articles and Speeches)*; vol. 4, *Doctor Zhivago*—the novel and poems.]

C
Poems in Almanacs, Magazines, Newspapers since 1953

1954: *Znamya,* No. 6. Ten poems from "Poems from a Novel in Prose," i.e., from the *Zhivago* cycle.

1956: *Znamya,* No. 9. Eight poems; *Novy Mir,* No. 10. "Bread"; *Den Poezii.* Poem.

1957: *Stikhi 1956 Goda.* M.; *Den Poezii.* M. Three poems; *Literaturnaya Gruzia,* No. 4. Four Poems; *Teatr,* No. 7. Poem "The Actress"; *Literaturnaya Gazeta,* October 19.

1958: *Literaturnaya Gruzia,* No. 4. Four poems.

1961: *Phoenix* I. "A Poem," i.e. "Hamlet."

1962: *Den Poezii.* M.; *Grani* 52. Frankfurt/Main. Reprint of *Phoenix* I.

1964: *Den Poezii*. S.P. M. Poem "Red Glow" reprinted from *Pravda* of October 15, 1943.
Two poems of 1942, one of 1943; three poems of 1953 and one of 1957.

1965: *Novy Mir*, No. 1. Verse and Prose "From the Literary Heritage." *Yunost*, No. 8. Two *Zhivago* poems "Fairy Tale" and "August," and "God's World," from *A Rift in the Clouds*. These poems had not been previously published in the Soviet Union.

ALEXANDER TVARDOVSKY

A

From cycle "Iz Novikh Stikhov" ("From New Verse"), 1963–65, *Novy Mir*, No. 9, 1965.

B

A.R.S.P. (Anthology), vol. 2. M. 1957.

Za Daliu Dal (Distance Beyond Distance), 1953–60. Long poem. Goslitizdat. 1961. Sections of the poem began appearing as from 1953. Awarded Lenin Prize in 1961.

Stikhi Iz Zapisnoy Knizhki (Verses from a Notebook). M.G. M. 1961. Pp. 128. The poems are dated 1933–60.

Tyorkin Na Tom Svete (Tyorkin in the Other World). 1954–63. A long poem. M. 1963. First in *Izvestia*, August 19, and also in *Novy Mir*, 8, 1963.

Poems (long poems). M. 1963.

Sobraniye Sochinenii (Collected Works) in 4 vols. Goslitizdat. M. 1960.

Kniga Liriki (Book of Lyrics) 1933–61. M. 1960.

Sobraniye Sochinenii in 5 vols. Khud. Lit. M. 1966– . (This edition contains the following works: Vol. 1, Autobiography. Poems 1926–66; vol. 2, Long Poems. *Strana Mouravia. Vasily Tyorkin*; vol. 3, Long Poems. *Dom u Doroge. Za Daliu Dal. Tyorkin Na Tom Svete*; vol. 4, *Sketches and Stories*; vol. 5, *Articles and Notes on Literature*.)

C

1953: *Novy Mir*, No. 6. The first six sections of "Distance."

1954: *Novy Mir*, No. 3. Another section from "Distance."

1956: *Literaturnaya Moskva*, No. I. Sections from "Distance."

1957: *Pravda*, September 8. "On the Angara"; *Den Poezii*. M.
1958: *Stikhi*, 1957. M.
1960: *Novy Mir*, No. 5. "Distance."
1963: *Izvestia*, August 18, and *Novy Mir*, No. 8. "Tyorkin in the Other World."
1965: *Novy Mir*, No. 9. "From New Verse" (1963–65).

LEONID MARTYNOV

A

Poems 1, 2, 3, 4, from *Stikhi*, 1957; 5 and 6, from *Znamya*, No. 3, 1961; 7, from *Literaturnaya Rossiya*, No. 2, January 10, 1964; 8, from *Yunost*, No. 5, 1964; 9, from *Molodaya Gvardia*, No. 9, 1965.

B

A.R.S.A. (Anthology), vol. 2, M. 1957.
Stikhi (Poems). M.G. M. 1957.
Lirika (Lyrics). M. 1959.
Stikhotvoreniya i Poemi (Verse and Long Poems), in 2 vols. izd. Khud. Literatur. M. 1965. Vol. 1 contains verse 1920–60; vol. 2, verse to 1966 and nine long poems written between 1925 and 1964.
Pervorodstvo (Primogeniture). M.G. M. 1965.

C

1956: *Literaturnaya Moskva* I. Six Poems.
1957: *Yunost* 1. Six poems; *Moskva*, No. 2; *Novy Mir*, No. 4; *Znamya*, No. 4. "From A New Book of Verse"; *Oktyabr*, No. 4; *Moskva*, No. 7; *Oktyabr*, No. 9; *Znamya*, No. 12.
1958: *Yunost*, No. 4. Four poems; *Den Russkoy Poezii*. M. Poem; *Stikhi* 1957. M. Poem.
1960: *Yunost*, Nos. 4 and 11.
1961: *Znamya*, No. 3. Ten poems.
1963: *Yunost*, No. 3. Ten poems.
1964: *Literaturnaya Rossiya*, No. 2, January 10. Eight poems; *Yunost*, No. 3. Seven poems; *Den poezii*. S.P. M. Two poems.
1965: *Zvezda*, No. 1. Eight poems; *Yunost*, No. 7. Six Poems; *Den Poezii*. M. Eight poems; *Moskovskii Komsomoletz*, November 6 and 17 (four poems).
1966: *Zvezda*, No. 1. Six poems; *Znamya*, No. 2. Five poems.

VICTOR BOKOV

A

First poem is from *Den Russkoy Poezii*. M. 1958; poems 2 and 3, from *Yar-Khmel*; and 4, from *Yunost*, No. 10, 1965.

B

A.R.S.P. (*Anthology*), vol. 2. M. 1957.
Yar-Khmel. Stikhi (*Steep-Intoxication. Verse*). M.G. M. 1958.
Lirika (*Lyrics*). M.
I Polya, i Morya i Reki (*And the Fields, and the Seas, and the Rivers*). M. 1965.

C

1958: *Yunost*, No. 4; *Stikhi* 1957.
1960: *Oktyabr*, No. 12.
1961: *Moskva*, No. 5; *Yunost*, No. 7.
1964: *Yunost*, No. 8; *Den Poezii*. M.
1965: *Molodaya Gvardia*, No. 8. Long poem on war theme "River Svir" (1955–65), pp. 33–73; *Den Poezii* M. Six poems; *Yunost*, No. 10. Seven poems.
1966: *Molodaya Gvardia*, No. 1. Eight poems.

BORIS SLUTSKY

A

First poem from *Yunost*, No. 5, 1965; 2 and 4, from *Izbrannaya Lirika*, 1965; and 3, from *Molodaya Gvardia*, No. 10, 1964.

B

A.R.S.P. (*Anthology*), vol. 2. S.P. M. 1957.
Pamyat (*Memory*). S.P. M. 1957.
Vremya (*Time*). M.G. M. 1959.
Segodnya i Vchera (*Today and Yesterday*). M.G. M. 1963.
Chetiré Voyennikh Goda (*Four War Years*). M. 1963.
Rabota (*Work*). S.P. M. 1964.
Izbrannaya Lirika (*Selected Lyrics*). M.G. M. 1965.
Sovremenniye Istorii (*Contemporary Histories*). M. 1965.

C

1955: *Oktyabr*, No. 1. "Noviye Stikhi" ("New Verse").
1956: *Literaturnaya Moskva* I. Two poems.

1957: *Znamya*, No. 2 and *Novy Mir*, No. 7.
1958: *Stikhi 1957*. One poem; *Den Russkoy Poezii*. One poem.
1960: *Znamya*, Nos. 1 and 11.
1961: *Yunost*, No. 4. *Taruskiye Stranitzi*.
1962: *Literatura i Zhizn*, November 24. Five poems.
1963: *Yunost*, No. 12. Ten poems.
1964: *Molodaya Gvardia*, No. 10; *Den Poezii*, M. Poem.
1965: *Znamya*, No. 2; *Yunost*, No. 2 (six poems), No. 5 and No. 10
(eight poems); *Den Poezii*. M. Five poems; *Sphinxes* I. July.
Poem "Sins and Fears" and "The State Has A Law." Also
reprinted in the December *Grani 59*. *Komsomoletz*, November 3. Six poems.
1966: *Znamya*, No. 2. Six poems from book *Sovremenniye Istorii*.

ROBERT ROZHDESTVENSKY

A

Both poems from *Izbrannaya Lirika*. M. 1964.

B

Flagi Vesni. Stikhi (Flags of Spring. Verses). Petrozavodsk. 1955.
Moya Lubov. Poema (My Love. Long Poem). Petrozavodsk. 1956.
Ispitaniye. Stikhi i Poemi (The Test. Verses and Long Poems). S.P. M. 1956.
Dreyfuioushchii Prospekt. Stikhi (Drifting Prospect. Verses). S.P. M. 1959.
Neobitayemiye Ostrova. Stikhi i Poemi (Uninhabited Islands. Verses and Long Poems). S.P. M. 1962.
Rovesniku. Stikhi (To My Contemporary. Verses). M.G.M. 1962.
Izbrannaya Lirika (Selected Lyrics). M.G. M. 1964.
Radius Deistviya. Noviye Stikhi i Poema (Radius of Action. New Verse and Long Poem). S.P. M. 1965.

C

1955: *Oktyabr*, No. 1. Long poem "My Love."
1956: *Yunost*, No. 10. *Literaturnaya Moskva* I. Three poems.
1957: *Yunost*, No. 10; *Oktyabr*, No. 10.
1958: *Stikhi 1957*.
1960: *Yunost*, Nos. 2, 3, and 10.
1961: *Yunost*, Nos. 2 and 10; *Znamya*, No. 7.

1962: *Yunost*, No. 6.
1963: *Yunost*, No. 3 and 10. *Znamya*, No. 7. "The Nomads."
1964: *Yunost*, Nos. 4 and 7. *Den Poezii*. M. Two poems.
1965: *Yunost*, Nos. 6 and 11; *Znamya*, No. 3; *Moskovskii Komso-moletz*, November 6.

YEVGENY VINOKUROV

A

First poem from *Izbrannaya Lirika*, 1965; poems 2 and 3, from *Musika*; 5 and 6, from *Voprosi Literaturi*, No. 7, 1965.

B

Stikhi o Dolge (Verses about Duty). S.P. M. 1956.
Voyennaya Lirika (War Lyrics). Voyenizdat. M. 1956.
A.R.S.P. (Anthology). Vol. 2. M. 1957.
Priznaniya (Admissions). S.P. M. 1958.
Litzo Chelovecheskoye (The Human Face). S.P. M. 1960.
Slovo (The Word). S.P. M. 1962.
Lyrika (Lyrics). Goslitizdat. M. 1962.
Musika (Music). S.P. M. 1964.
Stikhotvoreniya (Poetic Works). Khud. Lit. M. 1964.
Zemniya Predeli (Earth's Limits). Introduction by Leonid Martynov. *Sovietskaya Rossiya*. M. 1965.
Izbrannaya Lirika (Selected Lyrics). M.G. M. 1965.
Kharakteri. Noviye Stikhi (Characters. New Verse). S.P. M. 1965.

C

1958: *Den Russkoy Poezii*. One poem.
1957: *Oktyabr*, No. 10.
1961: *Yunost*, Nos. 4 and 12; *Znamya*, No. 7. *Taruskiye Stranitzi*.
1963: *Yunost*, No. 1.
1964: *Yunost*, Nos. 4 and 10.
1965: *Yunost*, Nos. 5 and 7; *Znamya*, No. 5; *Moskva*, No. 2; *Voprosi Literaturi*, No. 7. "New Verse"—eight poems; *Den Poezii*. M. Five poems; *Literaturnaya Gazeta*, November 27. Two poems.

YEVGENY YEVTUSHENKO

A

The Russian and English texts of the first five poems are reprinted from *The Poetry of Yevgeny Yevtushenko*. N.Y. 1965. The Russian originals were taken from *Vzmakh Ruki* (1, 2, 4), *Nezhnost* (3), and *Literaturnaya Gazeta*, September 19, 1961 (5). The other poems are from *Nezhnost* (6), *Yunost*, No. 4, 1965 (7, 8, 9); *Yunost*, No. 6, 1965 (10), *Den Poezii*. M. 1965 (12), *Znamya*, No. 12, 1965 (13). "*Pismo Yeseninu*" was first printed in *Russkaya Mysl*, Paris and *Novoye Russkoye Slovo*, New York, without the first two stanzas.

B

Razvedchiki Gryadushchego (*Prospectors of the Future*). S.P. M. 1952.

Tretii Sneg (*Third Snow*). S.P. M. 1955.

Chaussé Entusiastov (*The Highway of the Enthusiasts*). M. Rabochi. 1956.

A.R.S.P. (*Anthology*). Vol. 2. Gosizdat. M. 1957.

Obeshchanie (*The Promise*). S.P. M. 1957.

Luk i lira (*The Bow and the Lyre*). Zarya Vostoka. Tbilisi.

Stikhi Raznikh Let (*Poems of Various Years*). M.G. M. 1959.

Yabloko (*Apple*). S.P. M. 1960.

Vzmakh Ruki. Stikhi (*A Wave of the Hand. Verse*). M.G. M. 1962.

Nezhnost (*Tenderness*). S.P. M. 1962.

A Precocious Autobiography. E. P. Dutton & Co. N.Y. 1963.

Avtobiografia. Flegon Press. London. 1964. Russian text.

The Poetry of Yevgeny Yevtushenko. Bilingual edition. October House Inc. N.Y. 1965. Contains 54 poems in Russian.

Vot Chto So Mnoiyu Sluchaiyetsia. M. 1966.

C

1956: *Literaturnaya Moskva*. M.; *Pervoye Slovo*. *Moskovskii Rabochii*. M. (August); *Den Poezii*. M. (October); *Oktyabr*, No. 10. Long Poem ("Winter Station").

1957: *Novy Mir*, No. 4; *Den Poezii*. M.

1958: *Stikhi 1957*. "Partisan Graves."

1960: *Oktyabr*, No. 7. Four poems, including "Humor" and "Moscow Freight Station"; *Yunost*, No. 12. Poems "The Nihilist" and "The Railing."

1961: *Yunost*, Nos. 4, 5, and 12; *Moskva*, No. 6. Poem "Honey"; *Znamya*, No. 6, "New Verse"; *Literaturnaya Gazeta*, September 19. Poem "Babii Yar."

1962: *Pravda*, October 21. Poem "The Heirs of Stalin"; *Komsomolskaya Pravda*, October 21. Poem "Fears."

1963: *Yunost*, No. 9. "New Verse": Six poems, including "Again at Zima Station"; *Moskva*, No. 1.

1964: *Moskva*, No. 2; *Literaturnaya Gazeta*, March 3; and *Novy Mir*, No. 7.

1965: *Znamya*, No. 1. "Trip to the North"; *Novy Mir*, No. 1. "Ballad About Poaching"; *Yunost*, No. 4. Long Poem "*Bratskaya*" (The Hydroelectrical Station at Bratsk"). Pp. 26–67; *Yunost*, No. 6. Two poems; *Znamya*, No. 12. *From Various Notebooks.* "Italian Italy"—Nine poems, including "Coliseum." Pp. 71–84; *Sovietskaya Kultura*, November 25. "Ballad about Perfection." *Literaturnaya Gazeta*, November 6. "Red Guard Patrol"; *Moskva*, No. 6.

1966: *Yunost*, No. 1. Five poems "From Cycle of Poems about Italy"; *Moskva*, No. 2. Long Poem "The Pushkin Pass."

BELLA AKHMADULINA

A
First poem from *Syntaksis* II. Poems 2, 3, 4, and 5, from *Struna*. M. 1962.

B
Struna (Chord). S.P. M. 1962.

C
1957: *Den Poezii.* M. Poem "Flowers."

1960: *Syntaksis* II. M. February. Five Poems; *Yunost*, No. 5.

1961: *Znamya*, No. 8. "Lyrical Verse."

1962: *Den Poezii.* M.

1963: *Literaturnaya Gruzia*, No. 12. Long Poem "Rain."

1964: *Yunost*, No. 1. Long poem "My Genealogy."

1965: *Yunost*, No. 6. Three poems; *Literaturnaya Gazeta*, November 27. Poem "The Word"; *Grani 58*. Frankfurt/Main. Reprint of *Syntaksis* II.

BULAT OKUDZHAVA

A

Poems 1, 2, 3, 5, 7, 8, and 9, from *Bud Zdorov, Shkoliar!* and *Veseli Barabanshchik*; poem 4, from *Syntaksis* II; 6, from *Yunost*, No. 2, 1963; 10, from *Yunost*, No. 2, 1964.

B

Lirika (Lyrics). M. 1956.
Ostrova (Islands). M. 1959.
Bud Zdorov, Shkoliar! (Good Luck, Schoolboys!). In *Taruskii Stranitzi (Pages from Tarusa).* Ed. by K. Paustovsky. Kaluga. 1961.
Bud Zdorov, Shkoliar!—Stikhi (Good Luck, Schoolboy! and Verses). Posev Verlag. Frankfurt/Main. 1964.
Veseli Barabanshchik (The Merry Drummer). S.P. M. 1964.
Po Doroge v Tinatin. Stikhi o Gruzii i Perevodi (On the Road To Tinatin. Poems About Georgia and Translations). Tbilisi. 1964.

C

1958: *Stikhi 1957.* Poem.
1960: *Synktaksis* II. M. Five poems.
1962: *Yunost*, No. 6. Three poems.
1963: *Yunost*, No. 2. Five poems.
1964: *Yunost*, Nos. 2 and 12 (thirteen poems); *Den Poezii.* L. Three poems.
1965: *Zvezda*, No. 5. Five poems; *Yunost*, Nos. 1 and 12; *Grani 58.* Frankfurt/Main. Reprint of *Syntaksis* II.

VICTOR SOSNORA

A

First poem from *Den Poezii.* L. 1964. Poems 2 and 3, from *Den Poezii.* L. 1965.

B

Yanvarskii Liven. Stikhi (January Shower. Verse). Introduction by N. Aseyev. S.P. M-L. 1962.
Triptykh (Triptych). Leninzdat. L. 1965.

C

1962: *Den Poezii.*
1963: *Zvezda*, No. 2. Four poems from cycle "I and My Friend Zhenya Kubik."

1964: *Den Poezii*. L. Two poems.
1965: *Den Poezii*. L. Two poems; *Den Poezii*. M. Poem.

ANDREY VOZNESENSKY

A

Poems 1, 5, and 6, from *Mosaika*; 2, 3, and 4, from *Parabola*; 7, 8, 10, and 11, from *Antimiri*; 9, from *Treugolnaya Grusha*; 12, from *Molodaya Gvardia*, No. 10, 1964; 13 and 14, from *Znamya*, No. 6, 1965; and 15, from *Yunost*, No. 6, 1965.

B

Mosaika (*Mosaic*). Vladimir. 1960.
Parabola. S.P. M. 1960.
Treugolnaya Grusha ("Triangular Pear. 40 Lyrical Digressions from the Poem"). S.P. M. 1962.
Antimiri. Izbrannaya Lirika (*Antiworlds. Selected Lyrics*). M.G. M. 1964.

C

1958: *Den Russkoy Poezii*. M. Four poems; *Yunost*, No. 4. Two poems.
1960: *Yunost*, No. 9; *Oktyabr*, No. 10. "Fire in Architectural Institute," etc.
1961: *Yunost*, No. 4. "New Year Letter."
1962: *Znamya*, No. 4. "Triangular Pear. 30 Digressions."
1963: *Yunost*, No. 1. "Italian Poems"; *Pravda*, October 13. Long Poem "Longjumeau"; *Znamya*, No. 11. "Post with Verses"; *Yunost*, No. 11. "Mayakovsky in Paris."
1964: *Yunost*, No. 7. "Hare," "Roman Holidays," "Silence"; *Molodaya Gvardia*, No. 10. Long poem "Oza."
1965: *Znamya*, No. 6. "Arrested Motion" and "Laziness"; *Yunost*, No. 6. "Neizvestny—Requiem," "Kizh-Lake," and "Six Strophes with Irony."
1966: *Komsomolskaya Pravda*, June 1. Long poem "Help Tashkent."

NOVELLA MATVEYEVA

A

All three poems from *Yunost*, No. 10, 1965.

B

Lyrika (Lyrics). M. 1961; *Korablik* (*The Little Ship*). M. 1963; *Dusha Veshchei* (*The Soul of Things*). S.P. M. 1966.

C

1963: *Zvezda*, No. 3. Poem "Dream."
1964: *Smena*, No. 5. Short poem; *Zvezda*, No. 10. "Verses"; *Moskva*, No. 10. "Verses"; *Molodaya Gvardia*, No. 11.
1965: *Yunost*, Nos. 3 (four poems) and 10 (four poems); *Znamya*, No. 3. "Verse"; *Molodaya Gvardia*, No. 12. Long poem "Hypnosis"; *Den Poezii*. M. "Hypnosis."
1966: *Novy Mir*, No. 3. "New Verses." Three Poems.

LEONID GUBANOV

A

From *Yunost*, No. 6, 1964.

B

No officially published books as yet.

C

1964: *Yunost*, No. 6. Poem, "The Artist."
1965: *Sphinxes* I. Ed. by Valery Tarsis. M. July. Includes three sections (2, 4, 6) of "Normal As An Apple" and "The Fourth"; *Grani 59*. Frankfurt/Main. Reprint of *Sphinxes* I.

IVAN KHARABAROV

A

Both poems from *Syntaksis* I. M. 1959.

B

To date I have not come across any books by Kharabarov.

C

1957: *Den Poezii*. M. Three poems.
1959: *Kazakstanskaya Pravda*, August 2; *Synktaksis* I. M. December. Five poems.
1961: *Phoenix* I. M. Five poems.

1962: *Grani 52*. Frankfurt/Main. Reprint of *Phoenix* I.
1964: *Den Poezii*. S.P. M. Poem.
1965: *Oktyabr*, No. 10. Three poems; *Den Poezii*. M. Poem;
    Grani 58. Frankfurt/Main. Reprint of *Syntaksis* I.

YURY GALANSKOV

A
From *Phoenix* I.

B
No books seem to have appeared so far.

C
1961: *Phoenix* I. M. Long poem "The Human Manifesto."
1962: *Grani 52*. Frankfurt/Main. Reprint of *Phoenix* I.

IOSIF BRODSKY

A
Poems 3 and 4, from *Novoye Russkoye Slovo*, May 28, 1964.
Text checked with that in (B). Poems 1, 2, 5, 6, and 7, from (B).

B
Stikhotvoreniya i Poemi (Poetic Works and Long Poems). Inter-
Language Associates. Washington. 1965.

C
1960: *Syntaksis* III. L. Five poems.
1964: *Novoye Russkoye Slovo*, May 28. New York. 1964.
1965: *Grani 58*. Frankfurt/Main. Reprint of *Syntaksis* III.

Notes

BORIS PASTERNAK

Insomnia

This 1953 poem was first published posthumously in 1965. It was originally one of four "Cradle Songs," which were to form part of the "Poems from a Novel" (*Zhivago*) cycle. Pasternak later decided not to include two of them in the group. "Insomnia," one of the two, is rather freer in form than the other *Zhivago* poems. However, it does seem to have the feeling of "Lara" about it.

Hamlet

This poem has not yet been officially published in any of the Soviet editions of Pasternak, though it opens the *Zhivago* cycle in all the foreign editions of the novel. This may be due to the religious (Christian) imagery and symbolism manifest in the last three quatrains. By early 1966, sixteen of the twenty-five *Zhivago* poems have been published in the Soviet Union.

"Hamlet" was, however, included under the title of "A Poem" in the unofficial *Phoenix* I poetry collection.

The poem, it should be noted, is written in trochaic tetrameter measure which, in this case, has a slow dignified rhythm corresponding to the deeply religious and philosophical tone and the intense lyrical feeling of what is, in essence, a poem of sacrificial ritual.

BORIS SLUTSKY

Horses In The Ocean
  Slava: glory, fame, renown.

YEVGENY VINOKUROV

Adam
  Oswiecim: a notorious Nazi extermination camp in Poland during the war. Also known as Auschwitz.

Autobiography

"My own Nestor": self-chronicler. Nestor (c. 1056–1114), the reputed author of the earliest Russian chronicle. He was a monk of the Pechersky cloister of Kiev from 1073.

YEVGENY YEVTUSHENKO

There's Something I Often Notice

Lines 25–28 are also to be found in a long poem, "Whence Are You" (1958), included in *Stikhi Raznikh Let*.

This early poem sets the tone for the ensuing decade. It is a call for "change"—"I'll break with all I lived with up to now."

A Career

A defense of the freedom of genius, whether in scientist or writer, against slander and stupidity.

"Tolstoy—Leo" is ironic. There were three Tolstoys in Russian literature—A. K., A. N., and Leo. But Leo was the only "Galileo."

Freshness

A lyrical appeal for spontaneity against dogma and routine.

The American Nightingale

First in *Literaturnaya Gazeta*, No. 6, 1961. Then in *Vzmakh Ruki*. Written when Yevtushenko was visiting Harvard in April, 1961.

Babii Yar

Babii: women's. *Yar*: cliff or steep bank. A place outside Kiev where the Nazis perpetrated a mass slaughter of Jews. No monument was erected on the spot. Instead, it was proposed to build a stadium. The poem proved an extremely controversial one. It brought out into the open the Jewish question in the Soviet Union. The poem has not been reprinted there since its first publication in September, 1961. Shostakovich used it in his Thirteenth Symphony.

Alfred Dreyfus (1859–1935): a French artillery officer, who was defended by Émile Zola when he was accused of treachery. After being sent to Devil's Island, Dreyfus was finally exonerated in 1914.

Byelostok (English, Bialystok): a town on the Russian Polish frontier, which formerly had a large Jewish population.

"The Union of the Russian People": an ultranationalist organization in the later Tsarist days. It controlled the "Black Hundreds" —gangs that instigated Jewish pogroms.

Woman and the Sea

Apart from love poems, Yevtushenko has written a number of poems in which he expresses compassion or admiration for women. In this case it is a woman's bravery and determination in stormy weather that is extolled.

"Texas jeans": "jeans" has become a Russian word.

The Song of the Overseers

This and the two following poems are all taken from *Bratskaya GES*, a long poem or rather a loose-strung collection of poems on various aspects of the dual theme of "belief and unbelief."

Bratsk: the site on the Angara River in Siberia, not far from Zima Station, Yevtushenko's birthplace, of the construction of the Hydroelectrical Station (GES).

The Overseers: they might apply to the Stalin era as well as to that of the Pharaoh.

Art

In this poem there is an implied defense of modern art in the context of the conflict of ideas which was revealed at the time of Mr. Krushchev's diatribes during the Manège Exhibition of December, 1962, in Moscow.

Saint-Exupéry, Antoine de (1900–45): French aviator and writer, author of *Wind, Sand and Stars* (1939), who usually wrote about his experiences as a flier.

Scriabin, Alexander (1872–1915): Russian composer of mystical tendencies. The composer of "The Poem of Ecstasy."

Moussorgsky, M. P. (1835–81): one of the first geniuses of Russian music, who composed the original score of the opera *Boris Godunov*.

Gauguin, Paul (1848–1903): French painter who abandoned Paris, civilization, and financial independence for a freer artistic life in Tahiti (1890). Since then a symbol of artistic independence and integrity. See also Voznesensky's "The Parabolic Ballad."

Skira: well-known publisher of art books in Switzerland. No doubt the Skira editions have been a revelation to many modern-art-starved Russians.

Dégas, Edgar (1834–1917): the French impressionist painter.

Cézanne, Paul (1839–1906): the great French post-impressionist painter, whose work was the key to Cubism.

Rodin, Auguste (1840–1917): famous French sculptor of "The Thinker" and many other works.

Fellini, Federico: the well-known Italian film director of *The Nights of Cabiria*, *8½*, *Julietta of the Spirits*, and other films.

Gorky, Maxim (1868–1936): the famous Russian writer. "Newborn" must refer to Gorky's story *A Man Is Born*, in which he describes how he had assisted at the birth of a child while tramping in the Black Sea region.

Mayakovsky

As in "Art," the poet identifies all his better values with the spirit of Bratsk. Therefore, Mayakovsky too! But the question that torments him is what Mayakovsky would have done in 1937, one of the worst years of the Stalinist purges. Thus, again, the issue of artistic integrity is raised.

". . . if that revolver had not gone off": Vladimir Mayakovsky (b. 1893) shot himself on April 14, 1930.

"Black Marias": also known in Russian as "Black Ravens."

Letter to Yesenin

This poem was read at a poetry meeting in the presence of the head of the Komsomol. It has not yet been published in Russia. Yesenin, "the great national poet," is here used as a symbol of integrity and, thus, as a possible means of "salvation" from corruption and stupidity.

Yesenin, Sergey (1895–1925): a lyrical poet of great poetic power and impact, the publication of whose work after his death was for a long time systematically discouraged. In the last decade, in particular, there has been a great revival of interest both in his work and personality.

"Isadora": Yesenin met and married (May 2, 1922) Isadora Duncan, the famous American dancer, when she visited Russia in the early 1920's. They visited Europe and the United States together (1922–23). Then Yesenin returned to Russia in August of 1923.

"As a scarf . . . to her death": Isadora was later killed accidentally while driving in an open car on the French Riviera. Her long scarf, streaming behind her, became caught in the back wheel of the car, strangling her.

In stanza 2, the poet establishes an essential difference between

Yesenin's Russia and his own. The former was essentially pastoral; the latter collectivized and industrialized.

". . . the war against the people": no doubt refers to the millions of lives arbitrarily sacrificed in the Stalinist thirties and forties.

"*gorlan(a)*": the (big) bawler. A reference to Mayakovsky, who had spoken of himself in "At the Top of the Voice" as such, i.e., *gorlan-glavar (bawler-in-chief* in the sense of a "tribune"). In the same poem he also takes a satirical crack at Yesenin.

Komsomol: Communist Youth League.

Komsomol leader: apparently a direct reference to Sergey Pavlov, the head of the Komsomol, who was actively involved in bringing criticism and pressure to bear on the avant-garde poets in 1962–65. Since then he has been appointed to a high security post.

Poddubny: a Russian champion wrestler who used to compete in the international arena.

In Memory of the Poet Xenia Nekrasova

A poem of compassion and also of sharp criticism of the stupidity of the "moral guardians." Nekrasova (b. 1912) began to be published in 1937. Her first volume appeared in 1955. She was also included in A.R.S.P. and in *Stikhi 1957*.

Ksiusha: the familiar form of Xenia.

Coliseum

Written as a result of the poet's visit to Italy in the summer of 1965 after two years of enforced non-traveling abroad. On the site of the Roman arena, the poet sees himself as a poet-gladiator who risks being sacrificed to appease the bloodthirsty mob and who condemns this aspect of the world.

BULAT OKUDZAVA

The music of Leningrad refers here to the architecture of St. Petersburg.

Rastrelli, Bartholomew (1700–71): an outstanding architect, who was responsible for the building of the Winter and the Anichkov Palaces and the Cathedral of the Smolny Monastery. He was the son of an Italian sculptor who was working in Russia and who had done the bust of Peter the Great.

Rossi, Karl Ivanovich (1775–1849): a famous Russian architect in the Empire style who built the Petersburg Senate and Synod, the Mikhailovsky Palace, and the Alexandriisky (now Kirov) Theater.

Childhood

The Arbat: a street in Moscow in the Frunze district. Also the favorite haunt of Moscow intellectuals.

Pioneers: the "cubs" of The Communist Youth League.

VICTOR SOSNORA

Midnight

Kolabakha: a regional word not in the usual dictionaries. A sort of bread.

Carabas, Marquis de: a character in Perrault's tale of *Puss in Boots*. An ultrareactionary person.

ANDREY VOZNESENSKY

Pregnant You Sit

When Voznesensky read this poem and "First Ice" in New York at the end of March, he had added two or three extra lines at the end of each. The new versions have not been printed to date. The versions in this volume are based on the 1960 Russian texts.

Wedding

A longer version was first published in *Mosaika*. The later *Parabola* and *Antimiri* are twelve lines shorter, a new quatrain having been substituted for the original four quatrains at the end. Here we follow the shorter text.

Taiga

First in *Parabola*. Text in *Antimiri* shows a number of variations. In quatrain 6, line 2, *migaya* (winking) replaces *nagaya* (naked), and in line 4, *Tolko kverkhu nogami* (only upside down) replaces *lepestki nagibaya* (bending the petals). In this latter text all punctuation is abolished save two exclamation marks. The fifth quatrain has also been split into two couplets. Our translation is based on the *Parabola* text.

Parabolic Ballad

First in *Mosaika*. Reprinted in *Parabola* and *Antimiri*. There are a few minor variations in the latter text—more paragraphs and a line split into three. The poem as a whole is a lyrical manifesto in defense of "the true artist."

Goya

In *Mosaika* and *Antimiri*, with a few capital letters removed in the latter text, upon which our version is based. A strongly alliterative and assonantal poem on the theme of World War II, with an allusion to "The Horrors of War" by Goya (1746–1828). Another example of Voznesensky's use of the allied arts (painting, music, architecture) for poetic purposes.

Second Dedication

From *The Master-Craftsmen. A Long Poem of Seven Sections with a Requiem and Dedications.* The poem is devoted to the seven Master-Craftsmen (Architects), who built the church of St. Basil in the Red Square during the reign of Ivan the Terrible. The Tsar rewarded their inspiration and labors by having them blinded, so that they could not recreate anything similar. The poem as a whole is a sort of hymn to the master-artist. It is also an appeal against tyranny.

Dated 1959, the poem first appeared in *Mosaika*. Reprinted in *Parabola* and *Antimiri*. In *Mosaika*, the poem ends with a longer *Epilogue* instead of a shorter *Requiem* as in *Antimiri*. There are other variations in the later text, such as the deletion of a quatrain in Part III.

The only variant in "Second Dedication" is the word "tyrants" for "Sultans" in line 6, in both *Parabola* and *Antimiri*.

Antiworlds

First in *Treugolnaya Grusha* as "An Ironico-Philosophical Digression" titled "Antiworlds." Reprinted with some purely formal variations in Voznesensky's fourth volume *Antimiri* without a title.

The poem demonstrates Voznesensky's intrusion into the world of physics as a background to modern life.

Karakoum (or Kara Kum): a desert in Soviet Turkmenia. Has some of the romantic associations of the Sahara.

Introduction. Open Up, America!

First in *Znamya*, No. 4, 1962. Then in *Treugolnaya Grusha*.

Not reprinted in *Antimiri*. The Russian text here is from T.G.
The T.G. text differs slightly from that in *Znamya*. In line 3 (T.G.
text), the image *"koronuiyou Emelku"* (I crown Emelka) replaces
two verbs—*"otmeriayou, kumekayou"* (measure off, grasp).

Emelka: Emilyan Pugachev, the notorious Cossack rebel who,
in the reign of Catherine the Great, claimed to be the deceased
Peter III.

I crown Emelka: according to Voznesensky, the significance of
this "coronation" lies in "exalting the commonplace" or discover-
ing the extraordinary aspects of ordinary people and objects.

The Beatnik's Monologue

The poem is dedicated to E. Neizvestny, the modernist sculptor
and the poet's friend, who was harshly criticized by Mr. Khrushchev
in December, 1962. Voznesensky has lately devoted another poem
to him—"Neizvestny—A Requiem" (*Znamya*, No. 6, 1965).

"The Beatnik's Monologue" was first printed in *Treugolnaya
Grusha* as "The Second Monologue. The Revolt of the Machines"
under the general heading of *A Digression in the Form of Beatnik
Monologues*.

The text here used is from *Antimiri*. It differs from the T.G. text
only in (1) the formal arrangement of the second half of the poem
and (2) the deletion of two lines "Women give birth to Rolls-
Royces . . . / Radiation! . . ."

Sirin: From the Greek *seiren*—a Siren. In ancient Russian letters
and fables a bird with a woman's face and breasts.

Khan Batyi or Batu (d. 1255): the grandson of Ghengis Khan.
In 1236–39, he overran Eastern and Northern Russia. In 1240–42,
he conquered the South and penetrated as far as Hungary. He
established the rule of the Golden Horde.

*Oza. A Notebook Found in the Drawer of a Night-Table in a Hotel
in Dubna.*

We print only Parts IV, V, and VI of this long poem of XIV parts.
The poem has been described as "The diary of a young physicist
who is enraptured with the splitting of the atom, with lyrical commentaries by the poet. . . ."

Part VI of *Oza* represents a dialogue between two antithetical
points of view, based upon a rhythmical parody of Edgar Allan Poe's
"The Raven." It is not, however, the first use of "The Raven" in
Russian poetry for purposes of satire.

In the lyrical commentary in Part IV, beginning "Is it the wind makes the head turn?" the poet offers his ironical comment on the Stalin regime.

"Mayakovsky's heart": refers to Mayakovsky's suicide. See also Yevtushenko's poem on that poet.

Komandarms: Army Commanders. Army rank in the early days of the Russian Revolution and Civil War when the word "General" was unpopular.

Laziness

Diogenes: the Greek cynic philosopher (c. 412–323 B.C.), who spent his time meditating in a barrel.

podshofé: from the French *chauffé*—warmed or heated up. Here, in Russian, in the sense of having imbibed liquor; rather drunk.

Six Strophes with Irony

agiotage: a technical word defined as the business of exchange; speculative dealing in securities; speculation. Since Voznesensky uses this word which most Russians would not understand at first sight, there seems no point in paraphrasing it to make it easier.

LEON GUBANOV

The Artist

The last two lines of the middle stanza would seem to suggest Gauguin as the model of artistic action. Compare Voznesensky's lines "He rushed off, forgetting the craze for money,/the clucking wives . . ." (*Parabolic Ballad*).

IOSIF BRODSKY

The Pushkin Monument

This must refer to the statue of Alexander Pushkin (1799–1837) in Moscow. Pushkin was, of course, shot in a duel. His fate, as well as that of Mayakovsky, has assumed a deeply symbolical significance for the new poets of today. It may also be noted that, on December 30, 1925, Yesenin's funeral procession moved toward the Pushkin monument. Yesenin's body was carried three times round the statue before the procession moved on toward the cemetery.

The Wheelwright Died

Gefest: Hephaestus (Gr.) or Vulcan (L.). The God of Fire, who, in his forge, was also the smith and armorer of the immortals.

"convoy Vologda bound": suggests a convoy of prisoners bound for the Archangel region.

"Judge Savelieva": a direct reference to the woman judge who sentenced Brodsky as a so-called "parasite" at his trial in Leningrad, February-March, 1964.

The Court Sentence reads: "Brodsky systematically does not perform the duties of a Soviet citizen with regard to his personal well-being and the production of material wealth, which is apparent from his frequent change of jobs. He was warned by the agencies of the MGB (Ministry of National Security) in 1961 and by the militia in 1962. He promised to take on a permanent job, but he made no decisions, he continued not to work, he wrote and read his decadent poems at evening gatherings. From the report of the committee on work with young writers it is apparent that Brodsky is not a poet. He was condemned by the readers of the *Evening Leningrad* newspaper. Therefore the court will apply the Ukase of February 4, 1961: to send Brodsky to a distant locality for a period of five years of enforced labor."

The verbatim Russian text of the Trial was published in *Vozdushniye Puti* IV. N.Y. 1964. "The New Leader," August 31, 1964, printed an account in English. Brodsky was released in the autumn of 1966, and has since been seen in Moscow.

G. R.

Addenda to Notes

"Mayakovsky" (p. 103): "the best and most talented." This quotation is from Stalin's dictum about Mayakovsky in 1935. Boris Pasternak in *I Remember* comments: "Mayakovsky was beginning to be propagated compulsorily, like potatoes in the reign of Catherine the Great. That was his second death. For that he is not to blame."

"Oza" (p. 209): "The Komandarms' eighteenth birthday." This sentence may be taken in a double sense. It refers to the Civil War period (1918–21) when many young commanders got rapid promotion. It can also refer to what happened about eighteen years later when, under Stalin in 1937, there was a terrifying purge of Red Army personnel, high and low, including many of the heroes of the Civil War period.

G. R.